THE MINDFUL HOME

THE
MINDFUL
HOME

THE SECRETS TO
MAKING YOUR HOME
A PLACE OF HARMONY,
BEAUTY, WISDOM AND
TRUE HAPPINESS

Dr Craig & Deirdre Hassed

EXISLE
PUBLISHING

CONTENTS

HOME AS A HEALTHY ENVIRONMENT

THE FIVE SPACES

preface

How would a doctor and a calligrapher come to write a book on the mindful home?

We have each had a lifelong interest in mindfulness in pragmatic and philosophical ways, and our professional lives revolve around the ability to be present and focus attention. Deirdre is a professional calligrapher, which has to be one of the most exacting careers for being able to give attention. Calligraphy has given Deirdre a means to use beautiful writing as an art form and to use the beauty of those words, and the decoration adorning them, to draw people to read and be nourished by words of wisdom. Craig is a doctor whose working life teaching medical students, doctors, the general public and professional groups has almost entirely revolved around the teaching of mindfulness. Craig's personal passion

for, and knowledge of, mindfulness has been used to develop and deliver programs to help people with stress and health crises, and to enhance learning and improve performance.

Our passion for approaching life mindfully has extended to our home environment. Our home is not grand, and we have not learnt anything about interior design or spent significant amounts of money on decorating it (or having someone else decorate it). We have simply taken care to create a space we feel at home in and that we enjoy living in. A place that is restful, that reminds us of things beautiful and edifying, and one that is also welcoming for visitors. It is our wish, in this book, to share with you the philosophy and principles that have informed our choices.

This is not a book on the basics of mindfulness seasoned with a little discussion about the home. Nor is it an interior design book, catalogue of artefacts, or a book on storage solutions. Yes, there will be plenty of practical suggestions throughout but there are other books that deal with those topics in more detail. So what is this book about? It is a book on the home seasoned with mindfulness tips and practices to help you create the living space you really want and need.

What is the mindful home? How can you create one for yourself? In addressing these and other questions we decided to break the book into various sections beginning with the philosophy behind it, then exploring the way that we feed the mind and heart through the senses, how we use spaces within the home, the practicalities of managing the home, and how to live a healthy and sustainable life at home.

In this book illustration is as important as painting word pictures so we have used some photographic examples from our own home along with other photos and illustrations from various sources.

We hope you enjoy reading *The Mindful Home* as much as we have enjoyed creating it.

For more information on the ideas in this book, please visit the website at www.mindfulhome.net

the philosophy of the mindful home

Philosophy is the love of wisdom. Wisdom is generally associated with the ability to discern or judge what is true, right or lasting. It is also associated with insight, common sense and good judgment. Deep down, whether we realize it or not, everybody is a lover of wisdom. Therefore we are all philosophers in our own way.

Why is wisdom important to us? Because it is, or should be, the very foundation of our lives and the choices we make — the people we choose to spend time with, the way we earn our living, the use we make of the opportunities that come our way and the environments we create for ourselves. If we choose wisely we are much more likely to be happy and healthy. If we don't choose wisely, then we keep getting opportunities to choose again until we get it right. It's a little like the movie, *Groundhog Day* — we continue to fall into the same holes time and again.

Why is wisdom, or philosophy, important to this book? Because it lays down the founding principles that will inform the rest of the book. Mindfulness and wisdom go together, just as light and sight go together. The former is a prerequisite for the latter. If we want to live wisely at home then we need to bring awareness into the process so that we can see and understand what is in front of us. Then our choices are more likely to be edifying, informed and practically sound.

We want to consider what home is, not just physically but philosophically, and even spiritually. Then, particularly if you are new to mindfulness, we will explore the principles of what that is and how it can inform how we live. We will then start to explore the physical elements that will express our deeper intentions and needs in building, setting up and managing our home.

What is the home for?

Socrates, held to be the wisest of
Greek philosophers, famously said, 'The
unexamined life is not worth living'. I am
not sure if we are taking too many liberties,
but perhaps the unexamined home is not
worth living in. So let us begin by looking
at what it means to be at home.

The journey home

Before human beings invented writing there was a rich history of storytelling, an oral tradition of fables, myths and legends that had two main aims. The first aim was to entertain by regaling ripping yarns of heroism and adventure. The second, and deeper, aim was to transmit the collective wisdom of the community. These stories were not necessarily meant to be taken literally but to convey wisdom and meaning through symbolism and metaphor. They were there to instruct and remind the storytellers and listeners of the laws governing human nature, as well as the natural laws governing the community and universe in which they lived. Fables, myths and legends were there to convey the mystery of things intangible and intuitive. Over time they were written down and became formalized and, eventually, codified into collections and mythological traditions.

A recurring theme of so many of these stories has to do with the return home of the hero. For example, in Greek mythology, after the battle of Troy, Odysseus spends many years on an arduous but relentless search for his home back in Greece. Perseus had many adventures on his way back home after killing Medusa. There are similar examples from other cultures and traditions. In contemporary culture we too have many epic stories about the return home, from slaves pursuing freedom in *Twelve Years a Slave* and *Roots*, to safely bringing home a soldier in World War II in *Saving Private Ryan*, and even that most famous of dogs, Lassie, in *Lassie Come Home*. The pain, vulnerability and isolation that comes with being separated from home is also conveyed in historical events such as the doomed expeditions of explorers like Burke and Wills crossing Australia or Scott crossing the Antarctic, and in painting too, such as in Frederick McCubbin's *Lost*, portraying a young girl stranded and alone in the Australian bush. The vulnerability and danger are palpable for those separated from home.

There are other kinds of stories as well, about an inward journey home rather than an outward one. These are about redemption and finding ourselves. Road movies and books such as *The Grapes of Wrath* are classic examples of journeys such as these, as are self-discovery stories like *Good Will Hunting* or *The Razor's Edge*. Following discussions with writer and mythologist Joseph Campbell, George Lucas represented the hero's journey in his famous *Star Wars* series of movies. Such journeys may be no less arduous or relentless an odyssey than those described in the Greek myths, and perhaps the inner journey is what the Greek myths were really about anyway.

What does it mean to be at home?

What has this got to do with a book about the contemporary home? Nothing or everything, depending on how you look at it. Nothing if we think of home as merely a place to sleep, a receptacle for our possessions or as no more than an investment opportunity. Many people look at the home in this way these days. But it has everything to do with the home if we think of it as something far more important than that. What are the heroes of these stories looking for in their search for home? What is the pain associated with being separated or alienated from home, or not feeling at home where we live or within ourselves? What is it we are looking for when we get in our car at the end of a day's work, or board a homeward-bound plane after a long trip abroad? What are we looking for when we sit down to meditate?

I do nothing but go about persuading you all, old and young alike, not to take thought for your persons or your properties, but first and chiefly to care about the greatest improvement of the soul. I tell you that virtue is not given by money, but that from virtue comes money, and every other good of man, public as well as private. SOCRATES

A CONTEMPLATION EXERCISE

Where do we start in terms of cultivating the home we want to live in? A good place to start might be to sit down at home at a time when you are unlikely to be disturbed. Close your eyes, settle for a time and then, in an abstract kind of way, quietly reflect on what you would see the ideal home embodying, not so much in terms of what style of architecture, floor plan or colour scheme you might like, but what qualities would you like it to bring out in you or to communicate to yourself and all those who enter your home. Take a sheet of paper and, down one half of the page, write the key words or points that arise during this contemplation.

Then, when you have considered this for long enough and there is nothing more arising, open your eyes and quietly turn your attention to where you live. Just look. Do this as non-critically, impartially and objectively as you can, as if you were a visitor walking in and seeing your home for the first time. See what arises. What does the place communicate to you? Now walk around slowly. What qualities and characteristics does your home reflect? What does it bring out in you? Write that down next to what you wrote before.

When there is nothing further arising, quietly reflect on what you have written. What are the similarities and differences between what you see as being the ideal on one side, and what you see as the current reality on the other? Again, do this in a 'discerning' but non-judgmental way if at all possible.

Each of us will answer these questions in different ways, but perhaps we could come at an answer from a particular direction. What comes with being homeless or not feeling at home where we are? Do we feel isolation, restlessness, insecurity, dissatisfaction, yearning or distraction? Perhaps this gives us an insight into what home, or being at home, is all about — the opposite of this. Potentially home is a place where we can be at peace or come to rest, where we can be ourselves, where we feel safe, where we belong, where we are free of the constraints and demands of daily life. It is also a place from which we can be creative and in which we are nourished. Our current situation may not always feel like that, but what is it that we really want the place where we live to embody? Yes, home is also a place for sleep and entertainment, a place to store things, and it can even be an investment. But is this what is really going to make us happy or lastingly satisfied?

Perhaps we never ask ourselves these sorts of questions, but maybe we should. Maybe we take too much for granted. Maybe we need to create a home for ourselves that fosters in us the things we want to bring out of ourselves and manifest in our lives. Why live in an environment that brings out in us what we don't want?

So, what is it that you really want? If you answer something along the lines of, 'I want job security' or 'I want a boat', then ask the next question: why do you want those things? Are they an end in themselves or a means to an end? Ultimately we want those things because of what we anticipate they will give us, such as, 'If I have job security then I can be at peace' or 'If I have a boat then I'll be satisfied or fulfilled'. States like peace, satisfaction and fulfillment are the deeper, unseen things we desire beneath the more obvious and superficial ones that are superimposed over the top. If so, then why not go more directly for the peace, satisfaction and fulfillment in such a way that is increasingly independent of possessions and external circumstances? Let's face it, such messages have been at the heart of the world's great wisdom traditions for thousands of years, and meditative practices have been used as a direct means of exploring such questions.

What is the aim of the previous exercise? For some it might be your first step into mindfulness practice, but one aspect of this exercise is to begin to see what lies beyond the physical trappings. Whether or not we are conscious of it, the environments we live and work in are speaking to us all the time. Just as with speech, the meaning lies beyond the spoken words — with a home, the qualities it embodies lie beyond its physical form. Just as we can say one thing and mean another, so too can a home be architecturally designed, decorated just so, and be in the best neighbourhood, but it might not feel like a home or foster the inner state that we yearn for. On the other hand, a person's speech may not be the most eloquent but when they are honest and speaking from the heart we feel uplifted by it. Similarly, it can speak volumes when we enter the most humble abode but see that it is lovingly cared for, it contains things of beauty and significance, and it simply communicates the character of the people living there.

Coming home to ourselves

A house is merely a physical form but a home is far more subtle and elusive. It is not that the physical attributes of the home don't matter, just that they arise from the subtle human qualities of the people living there. Get the subtle stuff right and the physical form will follow; get it wrong or ignore it and the physical form will not be

what we want it to be. If we can be conscious of the qualities we want to foster and express in ourselves then the physical form will fall into place far more easily. We would do well to have those qualities in mind right from the time we design, buy or rent a home to the time we furnish, decorate and use it.

So, what is home for? This book will take the view that being at home is a metaphor for finding ourselves — finding the core of our being. What is at the core or essence of our being? Well, if the world's great wisdom traditions have anything to say about it, our core is where we feel at home and is the source of qualities we could equate with true happiness, peace, beauty, wisdom and inspiration. It is also about the good things in life such as domestic harmony, healthy relationships,

good physical health and wealth, and if Socrates is someone to go by, the latter are dependent on the former.

If we are to be philosophical about the mindful home then we will want it to serve us on every level, physically, emotionally and spiritually. How are we to find our core and create a home that reminds us of the qualities associated with it? Well, that is where mindfulness comes in and that is where the next chapter will lead.

What is mindfulness and why does it matter in the home?

For a practical and a philosophical approach to life that has been around for millennia, mindfulness seems to have become quite a fad in recent years. *Time* magazine emblazoned its front cover with 'The Mindful Revolution' along with a major feature article on mindfulness in early 2014.[1,2] Perhaps if we can get a clearer idea of what mindfulness is we can also see how it might be useful in the home and how a home can help foster mindfulness for those who live in it.

There are many things in this modern, hyperkinetic, fast-paced world that make being mindful more challenging. Home and work environments are conditioning us into what has been called 'attention deficit trait' which, according to an article in the *Harvard Business Review*, is a kind of distractedness associated with black-and-white thinking, difficulty staying organized, setting priorities and managing time, and a constant low level of panic and guilt.[3] Of course, the panic and guilt aren't always at such a low level.

WHAT IS MINDFULNESS?

Mindfulness can be described both as a form of meditation and a way of living. A simple way of defining mindfulness is as 'a mental discipline aimed at training attention'. There are other implied aspects of it; for example, mindfulness-based practices:

- utilize the senses in order to engage the attention with the present moment

- foster self-control through non-attachment to transitory experiences like thoughts, feelings and sensations

- encourage an attitude of openness, curiosity, acceptance and being non-judgmental

- cultivate equanimity and stillness by being unmoved by, or less reactive to, moment-to-moment experiences.

Wonder is the feeling of a philosopher, and philosophy begins in wonder. PLATO, THEAETETUS

One of the ways we try to compensate for living in such a world is to 'complex multitask' (trying to do multiple complex things at the same time) which, rather than helping, simply compounds the problem. It actually reduces focus and enjoyment, impairs performance, memory, learning and efficiency, and increases errors and stress.[4,5,6] It's a lose–lose situation despite the fact that most people assume it is the only way to work these days. The opposite of multitasking is 'uni-tasking' where we give our full attention to whatever is the main priority at that moment. On a practical level this means when answering your emails, just answer your emails. When reading a book, just read the book. When talking with your spouse or children, give them your full attention. Being mindful in such a way is sometimes called the 'informal' practice of mindfulness whereas mindfulness meditation is called the 'formal' practice of mindfulness. The two — formal and informal practice — go hand in hand.

Like any skill, if we don't practise engaging attention then we will get worse at it. Training one's attention in a mindful way can be done: firstly, through the formal practice of mindfulness meditation and, secondly, through the informal practice of being mindful which is being present, attentive, open and accepting as we go about our day-to-day life. The cognitive aspects of mindfulness, such as acceptance, non-attachment and being present, also underpin new and effective approaches to psychotherapy in treating depression and a range of other health problems.

Why be mindful?

Do you ever eat your food without tasting it? Do you forget such things as where you put the car keys or, even worse, the car? Do you ever drive from point A to point B without remembering much of the journey in between or even recalling seeing whether the lights were green or red? Do you lie awake worrying at night? Do you miss hearing what people are saying to you at home or work? Well, welcome to the human race! You know what it means to be unmindful.

Being unmindful, particularly when we don't even know we are unmindful, comes at a cost. Among other things, it costs us enjoyment because, for example, we don't fully taste our food, or don't take in the movie we are seeing. It wastes time, for example by having to re-read things because we didn't take them in the first time. It is unsafe because we are more likely to have accidents. It is frustrating and leaves us vulnerable to anxiety and depression because in a distracted state of mind we are much more likely to get caught in the 'default' thinking of rumination or worry. It also interferes with communication, empathy and connection with those around us. In short, unmindfulness is not a good investment of our time and energy.

Being aware is a little like switching on the lights and seeing what is happening, whereas when awareness is not illuminating life it's rather like living in the dark. When we're living on automatic pilot it's also rather robotic in that we are likely to think and act in habitual ways whether or not they are useful. When we're not in touch with reality it's like living in a dream world that will never give substantial or lasting happiness and that keeps slipping away.

Mindfulness, on the other hand, leads to the opposite of what is described above. Think of the times when you have been most fully present — perhaps taking in a sunset, working with greatest efficiency, savouring a moment of intimacy, tasting an exquisite wine or playing with your pet. Life feels much richer, memories are more vivid, we enjoy the moment more, we communicate more perceptively, we function far better, our sense of time seems to expand and our appreciation of beauty is much fuller.

How to be mindful

What we practise we will become good at, for better or for worse. It's as simple as that. It therefore makes sense to practise being mindful rather than being distracted. Practising mindfulness can be separated into the formal practice (meditation) and the informal practice (being mindful in daily life). Although they are referred to as two different things they are really entirely complementary. The formal and informal practice go together — there is not much point in being mindful for 20 or 30 minutes when we practise mindfulness meditation then being unmindful for the other 23-plus hours in the day. Some background and instruction for practising mindfulness meditation is given at the back of this book (see page 227). If we want to be more mindful in our daily life then we would do well to practise mindfulness meditation.

The mindful and the philosophical attitude includes things like wonder, curiosity, openness and acceptance. Curiosity in the sense of being interested in the world, ourselves and the relationship between the two. We can't learn or understand something better if we are not curious. Curiosity is natural for children but we tend to dull this down as we age and as adults we are the poorer for it. Parents often report feeling frustrated when they want to get somewhere and their child is wanting to stop and look at things all the time. The parent's mind is pointing to the future and the child's is in the present. The parent experiences impatience and the child experiences wonder.

Openness is important because what is happening *is* happening so we might as well be open and responsive to life as it flows. Resisting the reality of the present moment only causes frustration and is an exercise in futility. Take all the times when, outside of your control, you have had your plans for the day changed for some reason. How does it feel when you are open to the change and how does it feel when you are not?

Acceptance is closely akin to openness and is important because we regularly become aware of things we find uncomfortable such as anxiety, worry or some event we wish wasn't happening.

ATTENTION REGULATION

Being mindful involves both attention and attitude. Using attention in a mindful way is called 'attention regulation' and involves three main aspects:

- **knowing where our attention is**

- **prioritizing where our attention needs to be**

- **our attention going there and coming back if it wanders off-task.**

If we are reactive and judgmental in response then we actually increase its intrusiveness, fixate our attention on it all the more and may impair our ability to respond in a measured way. It's not helpful. One participant remarked on this at a course on mindfulness for people with anxiety. She came to notice that the anxiety came in whether she wanted it to or not, but the less she fought it the less it escalated and the less controlled she felt by the anxiety. If we were curious then we would have learnt such lessons long ago. Paradoxically, being accepting, even of that which we find uncomfortable, reduces its intrusiveness and makes it easier for the attention not to be dominated by it. It also makes for a more considered response if it is needed, or allows us to authentically be more at peace with a situation if there is nothing that can or needs to be done about it.

Many people assume that we can easily 'blank out' our mind or get rid of unpleasant thoughts, feelings and sensations but this is not so. When we become reactive to a thought or feeling we dislike, we actually increase its intrusiveness. Even when the mind is still active, we can learn to be impartially aware of thoughts, feelings and sensations without being involved in them, even the ones we don't like having. It is like developing a more accepting attitude to them which, paradoxically, helps us to unhook from our attachment to them. This doesn't mean ignoring all thoughts but rather cultivating an ability to assess their merits more impartially

and objectively, and choosing whether or not to engage with them. In this way unhelpful and distracting states of mind dominate our attention less, leaving us able to engage more fully with work, study or leisure time. The ability to do this means that resilience, which is natural to us, is not undermined by the preoccupation with such mental and emotional states. The principle is simple but it is not easy. It takes time to develop this ability especially in the presence of the stronger sensations, thoughts and emotions which can arise.

The informal practice of mindfulness

Being mindful in daily life is about being present and connected to the senses as we go about our lives, whether at work or at home. Any of our senses can be used for mindfulness — touch, taste, hearing, sight or smell. The art lover naturally engages the sense of sight. The masseur engages the sense of touch. A person who is vision impaired will have very finely tuned senses, particularly of hearing and touch. The wine enthusiast may not have thought of themselves as a practitioner of mindfulness, but the focus and attention they use in looking at, smelling and tasting a good bottle of wine is like a meditation in itself. That smell of coffee which the coffee enthusiast treasures is a moment of mindfulness.

Of course, if we cling to or get preoccupied with the things we find pleasant, that can lead to distraction; it may become habitual and even addictive and as such is not so mindful. To be able to enjoy something when it is there, without becoming attached to it, is a big part of living mindfully.

There may be a particular sense we are drawn to, but mindfulness in daily life can be directed to any single activity through the relevant senses no matter how mundane: from showering, washing the dishes, vacuuming or cleaning your teeth.

Mindfulness has a lot of implications for other things like safety, learning and efficiency. If while driving you are looking at what is happening on the road rather than thinking about what you are going to do when you get to your destination then you are driving mindfully. If you are a student

AN EXPERIMENT IN MINDFULNESS

To put what we have been writing about into practice, take the next mundane activity you need to do after you put down this book and do it with full attention. Whichever senses are involved with the activity, really connect, so much so that you unhook your attention from any internal mental dialogue about the activity. You don't need to look for anything in particular, but just notice what takes place.

listening to the teacher, rather than the din of your own thinking, then you are much more likely to remember what is said and be able to learn. If you are focused on your work rather than worrying about the deadline, you are more likely to work efficiently, use time effectively, work with less stress and feel less tired at the end of the day. Mindfulness is the very stuff of life.

The mindful home

It's rather simple really. Any of the senses can help the mind to come into the present moment or, as the saying goes, 'come to our senses'. Unfortunately, much of the time when at home we are still mentally at work. Equally, at work we may still be preoccupied by things that have happened at home. A good rule is to mentally be at work when we work, and be home when we are home. Another good rule is to go through our day step by step, job by job, and moment by moment. This is living in real time rather than living in retrospect.

People usually are the happiest at home.

WILLIAM SHAKESPEARE

In time, the practice of mindfulness can put us in touch with the core of our being, which is generally covered with distraction and worry. But this core, even if we have forgotten that it is there, is content, at peace and at ease within itself. This is like feeling at home within ourselves and with our surroundings. This state of inner poise is when we are happiest — not necessarily happy in a way that is boisterous, restless or craving stimulation, but in a way that is conscious, creative and quiet. Such a state is a rare commodity in modern life and one that many have almost forgotten exists. Many of the things we are exposed to in daily life, including most advertising and news, disconnect us from this quiet but expansive inner core. Finding this space within ourselves can be helped or hindered by the home environment we create for ourselves.

The home can be a help or a hindrance in our pursuit of mindfulness and inner calm and contentment. If it is to help foster mindfulness then, firstly, it should be conducive to the mind finding rest in the present moment. Secondly, the

senses should be nurtured but not overwhelmed. Thirdly, there should be a quiet place conducive to practising meditation. Finally, we need to consciously manage the inputs we subject ourselves to rather than just be pushed around by them.

There are many other ways that a home can foster mindfulness according to the way it is designed, arranged or decorated. Does it engage attention, for example? As curiosity is a natural part of being mindful, and a mindful mind is interested and engaged, so a mindful home is one that makes it easy, and even compels the mind, to be interested and engaged. Items of interest such as books on interesting topics, artworks of meaning or demonstrating considerable skill, or architecture that draws you in and unfolds a story as you move through a home, are all examples of ways in which the home can foster presence and engagement of the mind. It nurtures and invites questions and exploration.

More on this later, but for now, sit back and have a few mindful moments, a few pauses — or what we like to call a 'comma' or a 'full-stop' to punctuate your day with a little space — and digest what has just been written before moving onto the next chapter.

Architecture, proportion and harmony

'Let no-one ignorant of geometry enter here.'
These are the famous words said to have been
inscribed over the door of Plato's Academy in
ancient Athens. Not many people these days
would think to have such words written over their
own front door. We might be more disposed to
have something simpler like 'welcome' or 'home
sweet home', and rather than it being written over
the entrance it is more likely that our welcome
will be written on a door mat. Be that as it may,
why was geometry so important for Plato, and is
it relevant for the modern home? Let's have
a brief philosophical diversion to find out.

Let no-one ignorant of geometry enter here.

PLATO

The universe is all mathematics and geometry

Although many of us will have been happy to see the study of mathematics disappear into the rear vision mirror of our lives once we left school, we may never have seen it for the fascinating thing that it is. This is probably more an indictment on the way it is taught than it is on the subject of mathematics itself. Mathematics is interesting because the universe is interesting, and the universe is interesting in large part because it is mathematical. This was as obvious to the ancient Greeks as it has been to modern-day scientists from Albert Einstein to Stephen Hawking.

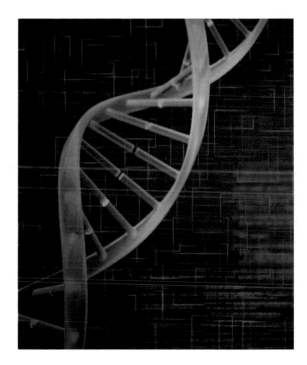

What is meant when we say that the universe, or nature if you prefer that term, is mathematical? It means that the physical laws which govern the universe — such as electricity, gravity, sound, quantum physics — are mathematical and defined by mathematical equations. The most famous equation is probably $E=MC^2$ but there are hundreds of others. It also means that mathematical proportions and relationships are always expressing themselves through nature. Music is moving mathematics, while geometry is mathematics applied to the three-dimensional world and the link between music, harmony and the universe has fascinated scientists for centuries.

The term 'geometry' is made up of two Greek words for 'earth' and 'measurement'. It is a branch of mathematics concerned with the shape, size, relative position and the properties of space. Thus, the universe is not just mathematical but it's also geometrical. There is no need to get too esoteric or to go into this in much greater depth here, other than to give a few examples from nature to illustrate the point. See, for example, the geometry of a snowflake or of seashells. For this reason the world's great wisdom traditions look at the universal creative process as being highly intelligent, organized, lawful and mathematical.

The golden mean

Whether or not we believe in God doesn't change the fact that, from the smallest to the largest scale, the universe is mathematical and geometrical. One particular aspect of geometry that occurs again and again throughout nature, and which was used at length by sacred geometers and architects, was what is called 'the golden mean' or 'the golden ratio', and this can give us a reference point when designing the proportions of our home. Mathematically the golden mean is approximately 1:1.618. What is special about this ratio? Well, it occurs all around us whether it be in the geometry of the nautilus shell, a galaxy or a flower.

The golden mean is also the basis of what is called the Fibonacci series. In this series, first take a rectangle of the proportions of the golden mean. Now divide off a square within it and then a rectangle of the same proportions appears again. You can then divide off yet another square to produce another rectangle, then another and so on in an infinite series. What you trace out is a spiral, the same spiral that is represented in the nautilus shell and many other works of nature.

The mathematics of this series is both intriguing and complex and since ancient times many forms of architecture have been based on these same proportions. One famous example is the Parthenon in Greece. The great cathedrals of mediaeval Europe such as Chartres and Salisbury are other famous examples. Architects in times

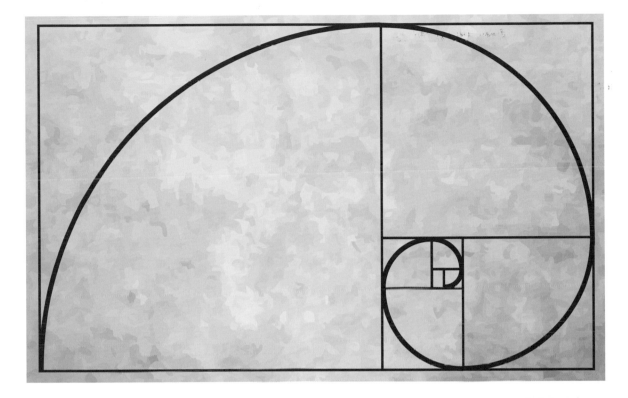

past, from East and West tended to have a strong grounding in mathematics, aesthetics and, indeed, the arts more generally. Before being let loose to design a building the architect needed to have an understanding of beauty so that they would build a beautiful building. Such beauty is both appealing to the senses but also to the emotions and intellect. Unfortunately, these days the love of beauty and proportion have been largely ignored or treated as an indulgence in the face of a utilitarian approach to architecture.

In the modern day there is a movement called New Classical Architecture that is combining the modern advances in design and sustainability with classical forms and styles.[1] Although it is an approach that has largely been used for contemporary public buildings, the influence of such architecture can also be expressed in homes. New Classical Architecture sometimes only utilizes decoration styles seen in classical buildings, such as columns, but the ones that take it more seriously also take proportion into far greater consideration.

We know it when we see it. When something is beautifully proportioned it just looks right although we may not be able to say why, at least not mathematically. Conversely, when something is out of proportion it looks odd, awkward and out of place. Some would say this is just a result of what we have been conditioned towards as a culture, but those with an interest in the mathematics of nature would answer that we have this geometry in our DNA, literally and metaphorically. The golden mean or ratio has an aesthetic about it, which is why it is represented all around us in ways we may never have realized, from the dimensions of credit cards and playing cards to the proportions of standard photos and widescreen televisions.[2]

In buildings geometry matters too. This is not to say that every wall, window or roofline needs to be based on the golden mean, but it is worth taking proportion into account when designing or buying a building. Although an architect may not have been trained in sacred geometry, they will often have an intuitive aesthetic awareness that reflects itself in the buildings they design. Before engaging an architect look at their other work. Have a conversation with them about their thinking on proportion and balance.

If we only look for utilitarian functionality in a building without consideration for the aesthetic then we will be the poorer for it. Yes, a house needs to be functional, but not *just* functional. Although we need functionality we are not enriched by it. It's a little like a doctor being medically proficient without the bedside manner to match. It doesn't leave your heart warmed, uplifted or comforted.

At home we built a straw-bale calligraphy studio for Deirdre where an old garage used to be. It was a simple rectangular space and we designed the building based on the simple harmonic proportions of the golden mean: the height of the building to its width, or the length of the building to the width, or the proportions of the alcoves carved into the walls, were all based on those proportions. Apart from the quiet and cool atmosphere created by the wide, rendered straw-bale walls, the proportions and the pitched cathedral ceiling give the building excellent acoustics and a meditative and tranquil atmosphere that many first-time visitors notice and comment on. A building can help or hinder us in our search for peace, but ultimately we have to go there ourselves.

Nothing can bring you peace but yourself. RALPH WALDO EMERSON

THE MINDFUL BUILDING

There is no one thing we can point to and say that it represents the 'typical mindful building' or is the 'mindful style of architecture' — at least not yet. The point here is to emphasize the importance of stopping to look; to be mindful when we look at, choose or design a building to live in. What is the effect a building has on us aesthetically and emotionally? What does it communicate to us and the world? What do we want to communicate? How does it sit within itself and with its surroundings? If we don't pay attention we may not know and our choices won't be informed or conscious ones.

Harmony

Harmony is another word derived from Greek — from *harmos*, meaning to join. It carries the sense of things fitting or joining together, being in agreement or concord. When the individual elements of a thing fit together well, as if they are meant to be with each other, they add value to each other, express harmony and create an aesthetically pleasing effect. Harmony is often associated with beauty. Without harmony there was no beauty according to Plato, and where there is no beauty love does not follow. In music, when notes go with each other according to the laws and proportions governing the musical scale they create a kind of harmony. When they don't go together we hear discord. In medicine, harmony is associated with health and disharmony with illness.

Many cultures have reflected on the importance of buildings being harmonious within themselves and with their environments. The ancient Chinese discipline of feng shui could be considered both an art and a science. Although one may be more or less interested in the metaphysical explanations for it, clearly many of the precepts of feng shui are based on common sense and

astute observation. There are principles for the alignment of the house, the use of light, the layout of the floor plan, garden design and the placement of water features, the choice of colours and the placement of furniture, among other things.

In a building, when the various elements work harmoniously together the whole is far more than the sum of its parts. In a village, when the various buildings complement each other, together they create a cohesive atmosphere and a sense of an interconnected community. One only has to go to the beautiful French or Italian countryside or to a village on a Greek island to have a sense of what this means.

On the other hand, in these days of postmodern architecture this harmonizing could be seen as conformity — a thing to be avoided at all costs. The main things that are communicated in the postmodern world of architecture and design are not so much the harmony of the thing within itself and its surroundings, but rather making a statement, novelty, size, utilitarianism, cost, individuality and, oftentimes, discord. It could be said that postmodern architecture, like postmodern music, philosophy or art, reflects the values and discord of the modern world. Often there is a desire to shock. It may or may not be right, or even possible, to say that postmodernism

is or isn't mindful. The point is that just as we want harmony within our body, which we can equate with good health, so we want harmony within the mind, which equates with mental health or happiness. In order to foster this it is useful to surround ourselves with objects and an environment that makes this easy rather than difficult.

The aim here is not to say that there is only one kind of architecture that works or is beautiful. There are so many examples of beautiful buildings and towns from every culture throughout history. The aim is rather that we take the time to stop and be mindful of the home we live in or the home we are considering buying. Does it communicate beauty and harmony to us? Do we even value beauty and harmony? If the building was a representation of the mind, is it a mind we would like to inhabit? If you are looking at the home you already live in and it doesn't communicate harmony to you, perhaps either move house or make whatever changes you can to produce an aesthetic you feel enriched by and at peace with.

The importance of things being 'beautiful and/or useful'

Englishman William Morris lived in the nineteenth century and was a textile designer, poet and novelist. He was strongly associated with the British Arts and Crafts movement and his work contributed greatly to the revival of traditional British textile arts. If you frequent such places as home decorating stores it is highly likely you will have seen his designs, or designs inspired by his work.

If you want a golden rule that will fit everything, this is it: have nothing in your houses that you do not know to be useful or believe to be beautiful. WILLIAM MORRIS

As those with large home libraries or wardrobes of clothes might attest, it is easier to buy books or clothes than to find the time to read or wear them. Equally, it is often easier to buy objects than to use them. All the time spent in shopping malls that seems to be so much a part of modern life has probably come at a cost, not just financially but in terms of cluttering up the home. Perhaps as a remedy to this, some people suggest that every time you buy something new, particularly clothes, you should relinquish something else.

Things being useful

If a home was valued purely for its utility it might resemble a cross between a supermarket, a hardware store and a whitegoods store with a bathroom and sleeping quarters off to the side — not particularly the kind of environment we would wish to live in. Obviously we desire to have things around us that enrich our home environment decoratively, that say something about the people we are and are a reflection of ourselves.

49

the philosophy
of the
mindful home

Things being useful sounds good but it's not always as easy as it sounds. Subtle differences in design can make the difference between something being a long-serving and treasured household item and it being retired to take up space in the back of a cupboard somewhere after only one or two uses.

We have often toyed with the idea of a book on all those household items that never quite perform their intended functions. There is the classic jug that drips. The teacup handle that is just a little too small to get your finger into. The spoon that is just a little too deep to get your lips right into it. The shirt not quite long enough to tuck in properly. The buttonholes that are just a little too small for the buttons. The outdoor umbrella that is only large enough to accommodate one person in the shade at a time. The back of the lounge that's just a little

too low and resembles a pillow more than a backrest. Designers should be mindful as well as customers. It's great if we can test things before they are bought but the bottom line is that beauty or adornment is an adjunct to functionality and should never be at the expense of it.

One aspect of things being useful is to consider how full to make the space in which we live. This will be discussed at greater length in the upcoming chapters, but suffice to say here that, if a space gets overfull   even if it is with the most beautiful or useful objects — it becomes a far less useful space and a far less enjoyable one to live in. This is not to say that we should live as Spartans or in a Zen monastery, but just to be mindful of when to stop filling a space.

A LITTLE MINDFULNESS

Now might be a good time to look around your house with that golden rule in the back of your mind. How many things can you see that are of no use or have outlived their usefulness? How many things can you see that are not useful but are meant to be there for their beauty? Do the items you decorate your home with uplift, nourish or inspire you? Perhaps there are a lot of objects in your home because of sentimental value, or because you have just grown attached to them and can't let them go? Would something look better in a place other than where it has habitually been? Don't forget to open a few cupboards and you might come across a few long-forgotten 'treasures' that would do well to be displayed or be found another home.

If there are objects that are neither beautiful nor useful then why are those objects still there if they don't add to the value of your life or to the utility and ambience of your home? Pause and reflect on that question. Reflect on what it would mean to pass that object on to someone who might find a use for it or find it beautiful.

Things being beautiful

If a functional object can be beautiful at the same time, then all the better. Indeed, many home goods manufacturers spend a lot of time and effort making useful items like crockery, kettles or ovens into designer items or things of art. Of course, when they become designer items then the cost can escalate. Do we really want to pay that much for a chair, a light fitting, a clock or a sink? Perhaps the first decision is whether we are buying an item of utility that we want to look good, or a work of art that has the bonus of performing some function. It is also great if those beautiful but functional things work together to complement each other, as well as being attractive in themselves.

It is really the things of beauty that create the aesthetic and tell the story of a house and the people living within it. There are many aspects to this. Firstly, in considering creating a beautiful home the decor, the choice of paints, carpets and/ or wallpapers is a good place to start. What do the colours communicate? What effect do they have on mood? Are they restful or energizing? Do the colours from one room harmonize with those on the outside and of the other rooms? Remember, the choice is not so much about what colours or designs stimulate or interest you in a showroom, but what do you want to live with for the next 5, 10 or 20 years? Also, remember: the more extreme a fashion the more out of fashion it will be a few years from now. (Of course, if you wait long enough it will probably come back

It is the things of
beauty that tell the
story of a house.

into fashion.) There will be more to explore on colours and what they communicate in Chapter 5. Pause to be mindful before making such choices. Yes, certain factors might influence you. For example, maybe there is a reason to choose strong heritage colours. Maybe there are certain council or local planning restrictions that need to be taken into account.

Secondly we can consider our choice of furniture. For example, do we want wood or synthetic, old or modern, plush or austere, classical or contemporary? Furniture can work well together if it has a theme to it, a style that is reflected throughout the house. In our holiday house we have continued with the white theme begun by the previous owner and given it our own decorative stamp with new furnishings, curtains and original but inexpensive artworks. This doesn't mean everything has to match perfectly, but if there are too many contrasting styles and colours then the home can look chaotic and anything but restful. You might love an individual piece of furniture in a showroom but it might not go easily with what already resides in your home. Furthermore, furniture is one area where form often dominates function in the designers' or customers' minds. A piece of furniture might not, for example, be comfortable or it might be

too large for the space. The issue here is to be attentive when 'trying it out' in the showroom so you are clear that you would happily live with the item every day. When you see something — a rug, piece of furniture, a painting — and you don't just love it but you know exactly where it will fit perfectly, then you know you are onto a winner.

OTHER DECORATION

Then there are soft furnishings such as cushions for chairs, lounges and beds. A single cushion can be a focal highlight of colour, texture and pattern in a room. Cushions also have a function for those of us with shorter legs or in need of back support. Equally, there are times when so many cushions are used as decorative devices that you cannot sit on the seat, or there are so many on the bed you cannot find a place to sleep.

Bookcases are also a wonderful addition to a room and can be a feature in themselves. They are not just for the storage of books but can be a wonderful place for displaying a piece of art or craft. For our own home, when we put on our extension, we chose to fill a whole wall with

a single bookcase as much for the aesthetic it created as for the function it served. We had to make a compromise on what style to have based on cost, but we have never regretted choosing to make it a feature. It can also be relatively simple and yet deeply satisfying to try your hand at making your own bookcases, albeit on a smaller scale. This can be a mindfulness exercise in itself.

Let's now turn our attention to artworks and artefacts. William Morris clearly had a strong desire to be surrounded by things that were there for no other reason than that they were beautiful. The right painting, carving, curtains, tapestries, rugs or piece of pottery in the right place can absolutely make a room. It will provide enormous joy if we take time to look at it and don't just take it for granted. It will also be a talking point for visitors, especially if there is a story behind the making, purchase or receiving of it.

Purchasing original works doesn't have to be expensive and it supports artists. Going to regional art shows, for example, can be a great way to find works by lesser-known artists and such works are often great value. Artworks lovingly made by yourself, family or friends add another ingredient beyond merely the aesthetic appeal. Learning an art or craft is a great informal practice of mindfulness, which is one of the reasons it is so deeply satisfying. Equally, a well-chosen reproduction or limited edition print may be far more feasible and pleasing than a more expensive original.

Beauty, as they say, is in the eye of the beholder, but we would do well to pause and be mindful before purchasing so that we are conscious of what the artwork communicates to us and whether we want that communicated on an ongoing basis. Many a time has an artist exhibited an intriguing piece that makes a strong statement or protest, but do we want to be confronted by that statement or protest every day?

Art or craft can be enjoyed purely for its aesthetic appeal and it may well put you in awe of the skill of the artisan or craftsperson. Even more useful if it uplifts your spirits with an ennobling message. It needs to feed the heart as well as the mind.

PART 2

the five senses

Although we commonly take our senses for granted, the conscious use of the senses is vital for our physical and mental health and wellbeing. In mindfulness terms, the senses are the gateway to the present moment and the world.

As with the body, the mind needs nourishment too, and senses provide food for the mind. We don't often think in terms of feeding the mind, but we should. Feeding the mind healthily via the senses involves both quality and quantity. We want lots of healthy nourishment: things that enrich, uplift, inspire, calm, interest and renew us. Fine art, literature and things of beauty fall into this category. Pursuits like mindless television and video games are empty calories and junk food for the mind; they don't have much value but are not too problematic if we only occasionally partake in them and don't make

them a habit. And, like cigarettes for the body, the toxic things for the mind are to be avoided as they provide nothing of value and cause harm even in small amounts. Things that debase or demean us or others, that are addictive or that sow ideas and behaviours that, in our more rational moments we wouldn't adopt, fall into this category.

Quality also matters. We might go to a Florentine art gallery and feed the senses on the most beautiful examples of Renaissance art and design, but by lunchtime we find we have had enough and need to do something else. It's as if we have overstimulated our sense of sight. On the other hand, we can sit in a bland, sterile office environment for many hours a day and yearn for some time in a natural environment like a park. So it is with our homes — we can both overdo or

underdo aspects which contribute to our sensory experience when at home.

The senses are our gateway to the present moment and hence to reality, because they only ever operate in the present moment. If the mind is off in some other place or time then it is senseless: we look but don't see, listen but don't hear. If the mind engages with the present moment through sensory input then it can be said that we have 'come to our senses'. The senses are central to the practice of mindfulness meditation and the ability to live mindfully in day-to-day life.

People are often more drawn to one particular sense. For example, people who love food and cooking might be more drawn to smell and taste. Musicians can be more drawn to hearing.

For others it could be sight or touch. It is ideal, however, for all the senses to be enlivened through giving attention.

Before beginning this section of the book walk slowly, quietly and 'meditatively' around your home environment and see if there is any one sense you connect with more than the others. Then, before beginning each chapter take another mindful walk with that chapter's sense in mind. Really connect with that sense. What do you notice? What do you experience? What effect is that sense having on you physically, mentally or emotionally? Note it and sit with your reflections for a while before reading the chapter. Use those reflections and the chapter as a springboard for making any changes you think useful.

5 Sight

Sight is probably the sense that is most obvious to us and therefore it tends to dominate the others. It's 'in our face', as it were. We navigate our way around the world with it and, for most of us, our spare time is spent with our faces in front of some screen or other — the television, phone, computer ... Although we take sight for granted, we would instantly recognize how much we rely on this sense if we lost our ability to see even if only for a short time.

The sensory apparatus that helps us to see — the eye — is, after the brain, probably the most complex piece of natural architecture in the known universe. The light comes in through the aperture (known as the pupil) and is focused by the lens and passes through a clear gel-like substance (vitreous humour) before it hits the back of the eye (retina). There it stimulates specifically adapted cells, called cones and rods. The cones are positioned at the centre of our line of sight and are most detailed and sensitive to colour. They need a lot of light — hence we don't see colour in very low light. The rods are at the periphery of our visual field and are less detailed but more sensitive to low light. We therefore don't see colour well at the periphery of our vision; but in the dark we are more likely to see things moving at the periphery of our vision than we are if we look straight at them. The optic nerve carries electrical messages from the eyes to the brain, and the brain then translates these messages into the image of what we are looking at. For this process to occur the brain needs to be working well, and the area most important for sight is right at the back of the brain. If this is damaged then we won't be able to see even if the eye itself is working well.

Sight and seeing

One of the striking things about sight is that we don't really see what we are looking at, at least when we are unmindful. The eyes and brain might be in working order, but if the mind is not engaged then we look without seeing. It's like the difference between a person looking at you vacantly while you're talking to them because their mind is off somewhere else, compared to them really engaging with you. In both cases the eyes are pointed in the right direction and images are being received but in the unmindful state they don't consciously register, whereas in the mindful or attentive state they do. The former scenario involves each person talking to themselves — one mouthing words while the

other is having a conversation with themselves inside their own head — whereas the latter provides the opportunity for meaningful, fulfilling and engaging communication.

You may also have noticed how much young children tend to see when they are out walking. The natural world is full of fascination and beauty for them, but for most of us, as we age, we generally stop seeing much other than the movies playing in our minds about what might or might not happen in the future, or replaying what has happened in the past. How dull and repetitive the world generally becomes for us as we age, whereas for the child it is full of interest and discovery. Generally when we think we know something we stop looking, but as English writer and philosopher G.K. Chesterton said: 'There are no uninteresting things, only uninterested people.'

The other thing about seeing is that we generally only see what we are looking for, interested in or expect to see. For example, if we are interested in books that might be the first and perhaps only thing we notice when we walk into a room containing a bookcase. If we are very self-conscious about having an uncleaned home, then when guests arrive we will probably see dust and lint everywhere but the guests may not notice it at all. If we are looking in our rear-vision mirror checking for cars then we may not see the bicycle coming up behind us. This is known as selective attention: we frequently look but don't see, or at least only see part of the picture.

Seeing the home

Sight is probably the first sense to engage as we approach home. We are likely to see it before we hear, smell, touch or taste it. We might be struck by the visual atmosphere of the house and the garden, or by the neighbourhood in which it sits. The architecture and proportion of the house and whether it sits well within its environment will be immediately obvious to us. Similarly, when we enter the home we will be visually struck by the atmosphere or ambience inside but by this time the other senses will have well and truly become engaged as well.

This is a start, but what are the elements of sight that are important to consider? The ones that will be explored in this chapter are: light, colour and beauty.

Light

The number one factor in relation to sight is light. It's the prerequisite. From a mindfulness and philosophical perspective, light is awareness or consciousness. Light is energy and the very source of life, mentally and physically.

We do not see without light and how we use light within our home can make or break it. A house may need to be dark in the middle of the night when we need to sleep, but an overly dimly lit house can have a depressing and dulling effect on us. A house which uses light well can invigorate and enliven us the moment we step into it. As far as light is concerned, there is the natural light provided by the sun, and there is artificial lighting.

NATURAL LIGHT

The importance of natural light cannot be overestimated not just from an aesthetic point of view but also as far as our health is concerned. Ignoring our health and wellbeing at home would not be particularly mindful.

The brain needs natural sunlight during the day to regulate the sleep patterns at night. It does this by helping the brain to produce melatonin at night, a hormone important for sleep as well as healthy immunity. Hence, a house with good natural light during the day will already be an investment in wellbeing and good health. If we don't sleep well then we are much more at risk of poor physical and mental health.

We also need sunlight for good mental health. It stimulates the brain's production of serotonin, a chemical (neurotransmitter) vital for healthy mood. If we are starved of natural light then we are at significantly higher risk of depression. This is a major problem in the winter months if we live a long way from the equator. The apt name for the tendency to feel more depressed in the winter months is SAD, or Seasonal Affective Disorder. The best therapy for SAD is sunlight with a bit of fresh air thrown in to boot.

We also need sunlight on our skin to help the body to produce the active form of vitamin D3, which is vital for good health and strong bones. Too much sunlight, on the other hand, is damaging for the skin. Depending on the season and time of the day, 5 to 10 minutes of sunlight on unprotected skin can give us enough sunlight to get our daily dose of vitamin D3. However, sunlight loses nearly all of its capacity to produce vitamin D3 as it passes through glass because the beneficial rays are filtered out. So take that 10-minute walk around the garden mid-morning or after 3pm and get some sun on your bare arms and legs. If you're going to be out for longer then by all means protect yourself from skin damage by using sunscreen and wearing protective clothing and a hat, especially in the summer months.

How we use natural light in our home is very important. We might not want direct sunlight coming in during the summer months for a variety of reasons such as overheating the house, or damaging furniture, artworks and wooden flooring. Double-glazing can reduce the heat problem and the use of blinds or awnings may be enough to let in some ambient light yet keep out direct light. In areas where direct sunlight doesn't come in you might want to have the windows unobscured by curtains or blinds and also by heavy foliage in the garden. That lovely glade-like atmosphere produced by the gentle shading of plants can become darkness if the garden becomes too tightly planted or plants become overgrown. Judicious pruning and thinning can help enormously. In the winter, of course, you might want to gravitate to areas where direct sunlight is coming in.

The size and positioning of windows should not be taken for granted. If you have moved into a relatively dark house then you need to consider ways to sensitively increase the amount of natural light coming in. Could you enlarge or add some windows? Would a skylight bring more light into a dark room? Can a lighter curtain fabric help to let in more brightness? Will the colours you choose to paint the walls help to make better use of the light that is there?

*Lamps are
the masters
of mood*

If you are designing your own home, preferably in conjunction with a good architect, then you can position the windows and glass doors as you see fit. You can also consider where the house will sit on the block of land, which way it will face, and where the sun's rays will come from in the morning and evening, as well as through the changing seasons. Also consider the climate in which you live, and how this will affect your choice to either minimize or maximize direct sunlight in some parts of the house. For example, a long linear window placed high on a wall will, in the summer, let in ambient but not direct sunlight, and can let in direct light during the winter months when the sun is lower. A deep eave over a window will also let in direct light during the winter but provide shade through the summer. Buying a house off a plan that is not suited or sensitive to the actual site on which it will be built might not serve you very well at all. It would be useful to have a conversation with someone who can help you make these decisions about the use of natural light.

ARTIFICIAL LIGHTING

The invention of the electric light globe was one of the greatest advances of modern technology. Mind you, there is still something lovely about sitting around an open fire or candlelight in the evening.

Artificial light gives us the chance to have the lighting as we want it and to enjoy the benefits of being in a lit environment after the sun goes down. There are many types of artificial light. *Incandescent* globes are traditional and inexpensive, and produce a warm yellow–white light, but they don't last as long as modern globes and require more power to run. They would generally only be preferred if really bright lighting is needed. *Tungsten-halogen* globes produce more light with less power. They are brighter, whiter and more efficient than the regular incandescent globe and they last longer, but they cost more. They come in high- and low-voltage varieties and can be very useful for highlighting and feature lighting. *Xenon* globes are even longer lived and operate at a lower temperature. They are very good for strip or under-cabinet lighting. *Fluorescent* lights may be an economical option and they last longer than many incandescent lights. They can take a little time to 'warm up' but come in a range of tones from bright white to softer tones. They also contain mercury so need to be disposed of in an environmentally friendly way. *LED* (light emitting diode) lights are generally small but more efficient and longer lasting than other forms of lighting.

The choice of lighting is not just a matter of what will cost the least over the short term. Over the long term a more expensive but economical and long lasting light globe will probably cost less.

Importantly, will the given light do the job you want it to do? What tone of light do you want? How bright does it need to be? If the lights we use at night are too bright then they can be aggressive and also impair our ability to sleep later on, as bright light at night interferes with the release of melatonin, the hormone released by the brain to make us sleep. Using the computer late at night can also do this and this is one of the major reasons for children sleeping poorly. To help soften lighting at night it can be useful to have dimmers. Alternatively, some carefully placed lamps can be a far better option than lots of downlights; they provide more options and can create a lovely mood, especially later in the evening.

Outdoor lighting is also important from aesthetic, safety and functional points of view. For example, brighter lighting and spotlights may be needed where there are steps and paths to navigate to the front or back door. More subtle lights might be better for entertaining areas or when you want highlights for your garden.

If wanting to revise your lighting options inside and outside your home it can be very worthwhile having a conversation with, and even a home visit from, a lighting consultant. It might save money, time and grief in the long term.

So, coming back to mindfulness, sit and observe the lighting and the play of light in your house at different times of the day and in different seasons. Be illuminated by it. Let it energize, awaken and engage you.

Colour

In centuries past, colours used in the home were naturally occurring but these days, for better for worse, we have a lot of artificial colours. Colour has already been mentioned in relation to light. Brighter tones are more reflective and very useful for brightening up darker rooms and making best use of the available light. But colour is important for many reasons apart from this. Colour is like the staple diet of the sense of sight.

The colours we choose for our home, inside and out, don't just say a lot about us, they do a lot *to* us as well. The effect of colour on mind and emotion can be subtle but profound. Colours evoke moods and are symbolically associated with various qualities and attributes. These principles are often better understood in marketing environments rather than the home. For example, the table opposite gives some advice for colour selection based on the qualities associated with that colour from a marketing perspective. The intensity of colour used in marketing and branding is likely to be far greater

than would be used in decorating a home, but the subtle message is still being communicated whether it is in the basic colours chosen for the walls, carpet and ceiling or those used for highlights in the artworks, ceramics or other decorative items we choose.

Colour sets the ambience or mood for a room and for the whole house. It wants to engender in you, or bring out, those qualities you want to focus on within yourself. For example, do you want a colour to help you feel at peace and to relax, or do you want it to engender passion? For this reason it is helpful to sit quietly with a colour — preferably a largish expanse of it — and see what it communicates to you. That you like a colour does not mean you will want to live with it or come home to it after a hard day's work. A strong colour that makes a bold statement may impress us at first but we are more likely to tire of it. Such colours are likely to be better for an accent rather than a whole room or theme throughout a house. Furthermore, the more a colour is in fashion the more out of fashion it will be in the not-too-distant future.

It generally makes sense to have continuity or a cohesive theme throughout your home, inside and out. You might want to choose one or two main colours throughout the house, and then mix it to different shades or levels of intensity for various areas. It can also be good to mix in

	NAVY	Generally considered a masculine colour associated with depth, expertise and stability
	BLUE	Tranquil and calm; the colour of the sky and water; it is often used to symbolize sincerity, trust, wisdom and truth
	GREEN	Associated with nature, harmony, safety, growth, freshness, fertility and restfulness
	RED	Emotionally intense, communicating energy, strength, power, danger and passion; visually striking and physiologically activating
	YELLOW	Associated with sunshine, warmth, cheerfulness
	ORANGE	Blends the energy of red and the happiness of yellow; associated with enthusiasm, joy, stimulation, creativity and health
	PURPLE	Blends the stability of blue and energy of red; associated with royalty, luxury, wealth, power and dignity
	BROWN	Earth; associated with genuineness, simplicity, dependability and friendliness
	BLACK	Associated with power, mystery, elegance, strength, formality and prestige; highlights other colours
	GREY/SILVER	Associated with dignity, wisdom and responsibility
	GOLD	Associated with success, money and wealth, comfort and quality

other compatible colours to accentuate particular elements and give a room its own personality while not 'arguing' with the rest of the house.

Also, check how your chosen colour will look in lighter and darker parts of the room and at different times of the day and night. It might well appear lighter or darker than you think and, accordingly, you might want to choose a lighter or darker shade.

Although a neutral colour throughout a house is safer it may lack interest and could need a lot of highlights to lift it. Colour profoundly changes how decor is perceived. A large room might need brighter or warmer colours to 'bring the walls in' and create atmosphere. A smaller room might need cooler or lighter colours to 'push the walls out' so that you don't feel closed in. Furthermore, we either need to choose the art to suit the room colour or the room colour to suit the art within a room. For example, a boldly coloured piece of art might not sit well in a pastel room, and a pastel artwork might not sit well on a feature wall painted in a strong primary colour. The art and room colours should complement rather than clash with each other.

CONFLICT

Conflict doesn't generally sit well with mindfulness, so we would do well to explore the subtle differences between the dramatic tension that can be created in a room of interest and creativity, compared with a room where all the elements are screaming at you (and each other) to be evacuated to a safe place.

Beauty

Beauty is all around us if we are mindful enough to see it. Ralph Waldo Emerson associated the love of beauty with taste, and the creation of beauty with art. It has been explored to some extent in previous chapters, but suffice to say here, beauty can and is experienced by each of the senses.

There can be beauty in simplicity and functionality as much as there can be in the highly ornate style of historical periods like the Baroque. There is a fine line between simplicity and sterility and unfortunately, all too often these days, aesthetics often lose out to utility, as if beauty were an indulgence.

Everything has beauty, but not everyone sees it.

CONFUCIUS

Things don't have to be expensive to be beautiful. Beauty has much to do with proportion and the way the elements of a room or object sit with each other. It is easy to think of beauty as being associated with perfection but, as Conrad Hall said, 'There is a kind of beauty in imperfection'. Some cultures, for example in Japan and the Middle East, are very conscious of this and intentionally introduce randomness and imperfections into their garden designs or woven rugs. Consider the simplicity of a Japanese garden with its carefully ordered randomness, the rustic charm and simplicity of a Moroccan house or the practicality and simple geometry of the traditional Australian colonial home — all communicate something of lasting beauty. Things don't have to be old to be beautiful, but reflecting on what gives such traditional living environments an enduring quality can inform us in the design and decoration of our modern homes. Things of beauty were created with care and attention — that is, with mindfulness.

6

Hearing

As with any of the senses, we would miss our hearing, our auditory sense, enormously if it wasn't operating normally. From a mindfulness perspective, the sense of hearing is a very important one to train and feed well, in large part because it is such a direct portal to the mind and our thoughts. In Shakespeare's play, *Hamlet*, the king is killed through the pouring of poison into his ears while he sleeps. If the play is about the inner world of Hamlet, then quite possibly Shakespeare is using sleep as a metaphor for the living death and vulnerability we experience when we are not living with awareness. It's best that we are mindful of what we pour into our own ears in terms of what we spend our time listening to.

Noise pollution and the modern world

Life has changed enormously in the last two centuries, firstly because of an increasing proportion of people moving from rural areas into cities, and secondly because the modern world has become more and more dominated by machines. As the twentieth century rolled on those machines increasingly found their way into the home.

The growth of industrialization and mechanization and then the arrival of the automobile profoundly changed life, in many ways for the better. But there have been some drawbacks, not least of which is pollution, including noise pollution. The sounds of birdsong and cows have been replaced by the sounds of the car, train, factory, washing machine, dishwasher, blender and, most importantly (or intrusively), the television. Many of these sounds are unwillingly and automatically thrust upon us as a consequence of living in the modern world, but many sounds we unwittingly choose for ourselves.

DEALING WITH DISTRACTIONS

Sit quietly and close your eyes. Pay attention to the presence of some obvious and persistent sound in your environment — it could be the air conditioning, the traffic noise or anything else you choose. Then after 20 seconds attempt to totally block out the nominated sound so that you can't hear it at all. After another 20 seconds note whether you are being successful in totally blocking out the sound. If you can still hear it then try even harder to block it out. After another 20 seconds stop, and reflect on your experience.

Most people will note that the 'distraction' became more obvious, and dominated their attention, the harder they tried to make it go away. This might have also been associated with frustration. Some people might not have been distracted by it, not because they blocked it out but because they rested their attention on something else to the point that they stopped noticing or being interested in the distraction.

The lesson is not to try to block out anything during mindfulness practice, but just to note that at any given moment there are thousands of things we could pay attention to, but we just happen to nominate or prefer one thing in particular rather than something else. It's more a matter of choosing what to be interested in so that the attention engages with that, and learning not to be interested in something else. We don't have to block it out; the intrusiveness of it will recede by itself. There is a lesson here for how we learn to manage environmental noise.

The auditory environment we live in can have significant effects on our wellbeing. For example, independent of other risk factors, exposure to significant road traffic noise at home increases the risk of heart attack by 23 per cent and exposure to traffic noise and significant occupational noise increases it by 57 per cent.[1] The reasons for this are related to the subtle but persistent activation of the stress response when exposed to high-level noise producing wear and tear on our body, called allostatic load. Added to this are the negative health effects of poorer quality sleep.[2]

Part of the stress is related to the volume and nature of the noise itself, but more significant is how the person reacts to the noise. Even relatively soft sounds can, for some people, have detrimental effects on wellbeing. For example, living close to wind turbines has been associated with poor mental and physical health but mainly in those with a high level of emotional annoyance and reactivity to the sound.[3] This is confirmed in studies that found pre-existing stress or sleep disturbance was highly predictive of negative health impacts associated with noise pollution.[4] The nocebo effect — expecting that something will have a negative effect on health and so it does — probably also plays a part.

MANAGING NOISE POLLUTION MINDFULLY

One of the benefits of mindfulness is that it can help you reduce the background level of stress; it can also help you become less reactive to, and distracted by, things that might otherwise cause stress. As a result, the emotional and physical stress decreases and you are able to better engage with life. The same has been found in helping people to be less impacted upon or annoyed by intrusive sounds including tinnitus, a persistent ringing in the ears.[5,6,7]

A key to managing noise distractions mindfully is not so much a matter of trying to block them out but rather preferring to be less interested in them, as you discovered in the exercise on page 80.

WORKING WITH DISTRACTIONS

One of the things that is most often a source of frustration for people learning mindfulness is the belief that one can, and needs to, block out 'distractions' in the environment such as sounds or things going on within us like thoughts or sensations. The extent to which our attention is drawn to, or influenced by, such things is called distractor influence. It is an issue not just during mindfulness meditation but also at other times, for example while trying to study with noise coming from the next room or while worrying about an upcoming exam.

Experience soon teaches us that the attempt to block things out only makes them more intrusive. A 'distraction' is just something happening, like anything else, but which we have decided shouldn't be there. We can therefore turn a sound from something neutral into a distraction and even a stressor. The effect this has on attention

LISTENING

Really listen. Listen to the sound of your own voice and that of others while speaking. Listen to the ambient sounds both inside and outside your home. Listen to your children, your spouse or your flatmates. Listen while you work. Listen to the music you play or to what you are watching on the television. Listen to the silence beyond the sounds. Listen as far into the distance as you can at night.

is for us to subtly monitor the environment to see if the distraction is still there and whether we have successfully blocked it out yet. Then the distraction becomes even more intrusive because we have turned it into a magnet for the attention, making it harder for the attention to rest on whatever we intend it to rest on. The solution? Let's not put any pressure on ourselves to block anything out or to make distractions go away. In fact, let's not even label anything as a distraction in the first place.

Creating the sound environment we need

It is not necessarily helpful to try to drown out noise pollution with louder sounds. There are a range of other things that can help to reduce noise pollution including: using fencing and noise barriers around our home, utilizing urban green spaces, installing double-glazed windows, using earplugs when necessary, and choosing carefully where to live e.g. not living near a main road or intersection.

We can and should be proactive in creating the sound environment we need. What kind of sound environment would we want to create at home? One that is conducive to our wellbeing and gives us more of what we want (peace, calm, happiness, lightness of being) and less of what we don't want (stress, agitation, displeasure, burden).

Again, taking the time to be mindful of the environment we currently live in will be useful. Notice the sounds and their effects on you physically and emotionally. Is the television on all the time when you don't need it or when you are not really watching it? Do you have the music turned up too loud? Noisy actions are a clear sign of an inattentive mind. Do you bang and crash things as you move about the house? Is there any place of quietude in the house? Are you comfortable with silence, and if not, why not?

Creating a conducive sound environment involves removing the sounds we don't need and then introducing the sounds we do. Obviously there are necessary sounds that are a part of life such as the sound of the motor mower on a weekend afternoon, or the fridge humming away in the night, or the washing machine. Yes, we can choose the time they are active or have machines that are quieter but it would be difficult to eliminate them entirely. Indeed, the sounds of family life have their own rhythm and beauty if we but mindfully listen to them.

The real problem is that we often make more noise than we need to because we are not paying attention. Some of the common modern infatuations include the pointless distraction of playing loud music while studying, having the television on without anyone really watching,

having emails pinging away when we don't need to be working, and people mouthing words without anyone really listening.

Life without awareness resembles what Shakespeare described as 'sound and fury, signifying nothing'. So pay attention to the sound environment you currently live in and see what unnecessary sounds you can do without. That will then leave space for two things: the sounds you might need more of, like the sounds of nature and soothing music, and a little more silence.

THE SOUNDS OF NATURE

The first thing we notice about modern life, particularly in urban environments, is that we might not have access to, or have stopped listening to, the sounds of the natural world. Even when birds are singing, the rain is tapping

away on the roof or the breeze is gently rustling through the leaves, we often drown it out or spend nearly all our time listening to the incessant chatter in our heads that psychologists have called 'default mental activity'. It's the stuff of distraction and worry, and when it is very negative it is the poison we pour into our ears in the form of negative and destructive thoughts.

We would be better off spending less time listening to that and more time listening to the heartbeat of the life around us. Two things will happen as a result. Firstly, we will feel less stressed, and secondly, we will rediscover something that was familiar to us as a child: what a rich natural soundscape we live in. To do this we will need to get outside more, something that happens less and less as screen time increasingly dominates leisure time. For example, an early morning walk or jog is a rich time for sounds. No earplugs, just the sounds of the birds waking up, the breeze gently blowing or a possum running along the top of a fence, along with the occasional car sound arising from and returning to the silence of the early morning. The physical exercise is good, but the benefit that comes from the simplicity of a little quiet and solitude is even better.

We can also introduce ambient sounds into the environment like the trickle of running water from a water feature or the sound of wind chimes. You don't necessarily want to overdo it, but these can be restful when not too loud and not used continuously.

MUSIC

It is a very good thing indeed to listen to music mindfully, as a meditative exercise. What is even better, if we have the time and inclination, is to play a musical instrument ourselves. We then get the benefit of hearing it along with the far greater benefit of being fully in the moment in the playing of it. Playing an instrument is a great way to focus attention, clear the cluttered mind and exercise the brain.

Music has long been known to have a profound effect upon our mental and emotional state. Plato in Book III of *The Republic* states how important he thought it was:

Musical training is a more potent instrument than any other, because rhythm and harmony find their way into the inward places of the soul; on which they mightily fasten, imparting grace and making the soul of him who is rightly educated graceful.

The trouble with music, as with food, is that what appeals to our taste and what is healthy for us can be two entirely different things. Although we might have become habituated to a particular type of music, we might never have reflected much, if at all, on how it affects us physically, emotionally or mentally. The therapeutic effects of harmonious and soothing music include:

- **relaxation, and pain and symptom management**

- **reducing cardiac reactivity and improving performance**

- **reducing anxiety and stress**

- **improved cognitive function (in the elderly, young adults and children) and mental clarity**

- **improved mood, cardiac and respiratory function for critically ill patients**

- **brain (EEG) changes and reduced stress hormones**

- **increased empathy**

- **enhanced immunity and increased melatonin levels.**

Not all music has been shown to have positive or therapeutic effects. Grunge, for example, has been found to have a negative effect on adolescent mental health with increased hostility, sadness, tension and fatigue, and decreased caring, relaxation, mental clarity and vigour.[8] Conversely, music designed to soothe was associated with the opposite of these effects. Doubtless, music of various types can have significant effects on emotions, behaviours and states of attention. But it is one thing for the research to say that meditative music has a settling and stress-relieving

effect on our minds and bodies, and that heavy metal, techno or aggressive music has the opposite effect; it is another thing for us to be aware of this for ourselves. We would do well to mindfully choose the kinds of music that bring out more of what we want. How do we do that? Following is another mindfulness experiment in noticing the effects of music generally and different types of music in particular. It may be a good basis upon which to make conscious and intentional music choices that foster the states we want more of.

What this exercise might help us to do is to be aware of the subtle but profound effect of music on our mental, emotional and physical states so that the choices of what we include in our home's soundscape can be more conscious and informed. This can also be a good exercise to do with your children if they are interested to try it.

LISTENING TO MUSIC

You might like to do this exercise with just one piece of music or you may want to have three or four pieces of music ready if you wish to reflect on the effects of different types of music. For example, you might like to choose something meditative like shakuhachi flute or Gregorian chant; something classical like a slower movement of Mozart or Bach; something like folk music or more contemporary but still harmonious and relatively quiet; something more up-tempo but happy; and even something more up-tempo and aggressive. If you are playing a few pieces then you might want to progress from the most up-tempo or aggressive to the quietest and most meditative.

The aim of this exercise is not so much to praise or condemn any particular type of music but to increase your awareness of the impact of music on the state of mind (thoughts and emotions), body, behaviour and attention. Notice this as you listen to each piece of music. It is also helpful to be aware of preconceived ideas about musical likes and dislikes and to let those go, otherwise we won't be listening to the music so much as to an internal dialogue about the music. Simply listen to the music on its merits, and non-judgmentally notice its effect. Ensure that when the music is played the volume is clearly audible but not so loud that you get a shock when the music begins.

This exercise can be practised sitting up or lying down. If lying down ensure you are comfortable. When settled, take a few minutes for a brief body scan (see page 228), preferably with the eyes closed. Then engage your attention with the sense of hearing, initially with any ambient sounds, before starting the music. Throughout the listening period with the music, let your attention be contemplative, with the music as the focus of attention. There is no need to block out anything else, but simply notice when the attention wanders from the music and gently re-engage the attention with it.

After each piece of music is completed, reflect on what you noticed about its effect on your mind, body and attention. Did it or did it not give rise to peace, calm or clarity? Did it give rise to any particular emotions, impulses or behaviours? Were they states or experiences that you want more of in your life or not?

SILENCE

What a rare commodity silence is these days, but how important it is. If you have experienced both the quiet of deep meditation and the uneasiness of a couple not on speaking terms, you will know there are different kinds of silence. What is the main difference between these two kinds of silence? In the former there is real silence, within as well as without. In such a state — the most beautiful form of peace and quiet we can experience — the mind is quiet, or at least we are not moved by the movements in the mind. As a result there is a sense of being at one with ourselves and with the world around us. In the latter there is silence on the outside but generally the noise of a seething mind on the inside. Such a state is inwardly full of conflict and division, with the outward silence merely masking and suppressing it.

Silence is not something that most people find easy to sit with, at least not these days. One interesting study found that most people would prefer doing mundane activities and even self-administer electric shocks rather than sit quietly in a room by themselves for 15 minutes.[9] What does that say about us and our relationship with our own mind? Being quiet and by ourselves makes us aware of what is going on in our mind and most of us don't like what we see (or hear) and don't know how to deal with it. It is one of the main reasons that some people find mindfulness confronting. To deal with the internal noise we try to numb it, drug it or drown it out with incessant noise and activity.

Is there a better remedy? It starts with the inner silence. Meditate! Learn to be with yourself. Learn to rest as the simple but silent witness, even if the internal state is noisy. Learn, through non-attachment, not to get swept away by every stray thought going through the mind. We might not find it easy at first but it will get easier if we practise, are patient and are kind to ourselves. Turn to page 226 for a detailed guide to mindfulness meditation.

Then there's the outer silence. Create quiet in the home, or at least periods in the day when you make space for quiet. If you have the luxury, you might like to dedicate a room to quiet and contemplative pastimes including meditation. For parents, choose the food you give a child's mind even more carefully than you choose the food you give their bodies. This includes choosing the sounds (e.g. television and music). Help children from an early age to be comfortable with times of quiet. Although much of their day will be filled with either frenetic activity or sleep, children will take easily to inner quiet if they are given an environment that is conducive to it.

7

Touch

It's a tactile world we live in, from the fine touch required to gently tend a child's grazed knee, to the simple enjoyment of running your fingertips across the surface of a well-finished piece of furniture, to the intimate and caring caress of one's partner. How would we live without it? Not easily and not well. Then there is that subtle sense of being in touch, say, being able to read the feelings of a friend or close relative. In this chapter we will explore the role of touch and how we can cultivate it mindfully in the home.

Living mindfully with pleasure and pain

Let's get a little philosophical for a moment. Senses have a functional role, with one important function being to encourage us to do the things that are important for survival (generally things that are pleasant) and avoid things that might be dangerous (generally things that are unpleasant). So, burning our hand on the stove is unpleasant and we generally try to avoid it, whereas making love is pleasant so most people are positively disposed to it. Does that mean that pleasure is always good and that more is always better? Does that also mean that pain is always bad and should always be avoided? No, on both accounts.

Pleasure and pain are sometimes described as being the two banks between which the river of life flows. A problem arises when we get 'snagged' on one or other bank. What does that mean? Well, the warmth and softness of the blankets or quilt on a cool morning has to be one of life's pleasures, the enjoyment of which seems to be amplified enormously when the competing need for work or exercise beckons. If our reference point is what is pleasant to touch rather than what is necessary or healthy, then we are unlikely to get out of bed at all. We could phone the boss and say that in bed that morning we got 'snagged' on the pleasure of sleeping in and couldn't make it to work, but the boss is not likely to be very sympathetic. We could tell the doctor tending our heart attack in the emergency ward that we never get out of bed to be physically active because we get snagged on the bedclothes, but that won't alter the fact of them telling us that exercise is one of the body's non-negotiable needs.

The brain's pleasure or reward centres are important but they only have one reference point — more pleasure and less pain. But sometimes things that are pleasant are neither necessary nor healthy, or at least not in excess, and things that are uncomfortable may be both necessary and healthy. The pleasure centres are not able to make this distinction. That is the job of the areas of the psyche and brain with the capacity for reason and discernment (the executive functioning area or prefrontal cortex). If we overfeed the pleasure or reward centres and don't exercise the executive functioning areas then we find it hard to make good choices, and in the end we cause ourselves a lot more pain than we desired or anticipated.

Strangely, freedom lies in the non-attachment to pleasure and pain rather than the futile attempt to enjoy a life of unbridled pleasure. In self-mastery lies freedom and happiness. This has been well understood by wisdom traditions for millennia, but the widespread misunderstanding of this simple truth in the modern world is one of the main factors behind the increasingly addictive and depressive world we currently live in.

It is one of the key elements of mindfulness practice to be able to observe the constant flux of pleasure and pain with less and less attachment to them. That doesn't mean the abnegation of all things pleasurable, or the pursuit of all things painful just for their own sake. It just means that we can enjoy pleasant things when they are there without craving them, clinging to them or pursuing them when our better judgment says otherwise. It also means that we can better endure things that are uncomfortable with less suffering when there is a good reason to do so. This goes to the heart of self-mastery and living with wisdom.

Mindfulness meditation will teach us much about being able to sit without attachment in the presence of pleasant and unpleasant physical and emotional states. It cultivates a type of equanimity. But this has to be supported and deepened by our ability to translate that into our daily lives. We need to be mindful enough to be aware of what governs our moment-by-moment decisions and to choose wisely. It won't always be easy but the more we do it the better it will be for us and for those with whom we live.

Knowing others is intelligence;
knowing yourself is true wisdom.
Mastering others is strength;
mastering yourself is true power.
If you realize that you have enough,
you are truly rich. LAO TZU,
TAO TE CHING

Being in touch in the home

On a practical level, how can we mindfully feed, rather than indulge, the sense of touch in the home? Paying attention is a good start and our home environment is full of opportunities. There is enough in our environment already. When mindful enough to remember, practise being in touch, even with simple and mundane activities. Feel the crockery you are washing. Feel the texture of the bench you are wiping. Feel the pressure of the fingers on the keyboard or pen with which you are writing. Feel the touch of the person whose hand you are holding. Feel the weight and movement of the chainsaw you are using in the garden.

Why? For a start it will help to get us out of our heads and the constant flow of worry or preoccupation we are generally caught up in. We will find that mundane life becomes much more interesting when we mindfully shift the attention from the repetitive internal dialogue we have with ourselves about how boring life is and that we would be better off being anywhere other than here and now. These mundane activities will become much fuller and richer as life starts to fill itself with simple pleasures. Simply by paying attention, our work and actions will be performed more safely, efficiently and effectively, and less expensively. We will learn and

Fill your life with simple pleasures.

become more expert in doing something if we pay attention to it and the time will pass more easily. Furthermore, when your attention is fully engaged that's when creativity can open up. There is much to gain and nothing to lose by being in touch.

Feeding touch

It's a simple but lovely thing to be in touch. We take so many things for granted and rarely stop to consciously and intentionally enjoy the surface of that carefully crafted piece of furniture, the crisp touch of freshly laundered sheets or the surface of a just-washed plate. The point is to feed, not overfeed, the senses. The experience of a warm shower, especially after a run in the cold morning air, is a sheer delight. But if we are still indulging that enjoyment to the point that we are running late for work or have drained the town's water storage then we might be taking it a little too far. Notice, too, the habitual avoidance of discomfort. For example, the discomfort of getting out of bed in the morning is minimal and short-lived but it can create havoc with a person's life and simply plunge them into a world of rumination and set up a pattern of avoidance.

We can also choose to consciously bring things into our world that engage the sense of touch. Do we take time to feel the textures of the plants we put in the garden? Do we choose the craftworks around our home as much for what they can offer us tactilely as visually?

Children and the tactile world

Helping children to develop their sense of touch with experiments and exploration is a vital part of engaging them and teaching them about the world in which they live. Teach them crafts. Let them get their hands dirty planting seedlings in a vegetable garden or creating a worm farm. Play games that involve touch. Close the eyes and feel. Use the sense of touch when walking in the park.

One of the most unfortunate aspects of home and school life for many children and adolescents these days is that nearly all the tactile experiences that were once a normal part of growing up have been replaced by virtual, on-screen experiences. No wonder many children are so easily bored and find it hard to engage attention for long with anything that is not screaming at them.

Young children are naturally curious and their world is full of new experiences and sensations — all day long. It could be seen as sensory overload except that it is all fresh and in the moment for them. They absorb experience like a sponge.

8

Smell

In many ways smell — the olfactory sense — is the most neglected of the five senses. The others tend to dominate so much that the sense of smell often remains underdeveloped or underutilized. This means that we could be missing out on a lot and there is room for improvement.

Smells are carried by the air. Fresh air is just air without anything else added to it. The smells we experience are small particles (molecules, chemicals) carried by the air that act on the lining of the nose. Smell is very important for the sense of taste, for if smell is not working then the sense of taste is much duller. Furthermore, people who lose the sense of smell easily become depressed, not having realized how important the sense was.

The smells of everyday life

There are some smells we make an effort to smell: that bottle of fine red wine, the new fragrance we paid so much money for, the soap or scented candle we spent some time choosing at the craft market. But also think how much poorer our life would be without the simple aromas of everyday life we so often take for granted. These are the unsung heroes of domestic bliss: the smell of freshly baked bread, the aroma of brewing coffee (for those who drink it), the fragrance of freshly cut grass or jasmine in bloom, the scent of newly washed hands, the smell of freshly chopped herbs in the kitchen. They arise without any fanfare and are fleetingly noted somewhere in the dark recesses of our consciousness as we unceasingly go about life. We don't often take time to stop and smell the roses.

Then, of course, there are the smells of neglect and stagnation — the unopened, dark and dusty room, the unemptied rubbish bin or compost bucket, the stagnant water in the vase of flowers long past their use-by date. Again, they linger briefly in our awareness as they are passed over. Perhaps they need to get to the point where we can't ignore them any more before they get our attention and we act upon them.

We often don't notice smells because we become habituated to them. The sense of smell becomes insensitive to scents it experiences persistently. Those visiting the New Zealand city of Rotorua or Yellowstone National Park in the United States for the first time will be almost overcome by the pungent smells of sulphur from geothermal activity and boiling mud pools. But once we have been there for some time we won't notice the smell much at all. Then there are the sweaty gym clothes and body odour that we stop noticing after a while. This is, in part, related to being less attentive to something through familiarity (which happens to the other senses as well), but also the sense of smell becomes fatigued in relation to a particular scent so it is no longer noticed.

Our nose informs us in so many ways that are overlooked, so let's take some time to consider some of the main issues and factors in relation to the sense of smell.

SMELLING WITH AWARENESS

The home environment is rich in olfactory experiences. Like any of the senses, we can do much to shape the sense of smell to our needs and liking. But the first step is to note mindfully what is already there. So take a little time to go into various rooms of your home and also outdoors. As the saying goes, stop and smell the roses or whatever else there is to be smelled.

Your nose will be most receptive to the smells of your house if you have been out and away from home for a little while. When you open the front door, stop and take a couple of slow, deep and deliberate in-breaths through the nose. What do you note? What does it say to you? What is the effect of what you smell? Move through the house and do the same thing. Does the kitchen smell different to the bathroom or bedrooms? You might notice the scent of ripe fruit in a kitchen bowl. You might notice a newly opened cake of soap or a musty shower in the bathroom. Then go out into the garden. Is there anything you would change? How would you best do that?

Fresh air

Depending on which way you look at it, nature loves or hates stagnation. Water that is not flowing or replenished becomes stagnant and infected and is a breeding environment for mosquitoes. It is not dissimilar with air. In order to stay healthy, air needs to keep flowing as well. Yet achieving this within your home might not always be easy or practical; for example, throwing open all the windows in the depths of a Canadian or northern European winter, or in the middle of an Australian summer, is neither comfortable, energy efficient or safe. But all things being equal, it is very useful whenever possible to encourage a flow of fresh air to replenish the atmosphere in your home whether by an open window, extraction fans or keeping doors open. This flow of fresh air will also be useful for reducing the chances of passing on respiratory or other infections as well as reducing problems with damp and mould. You might also have noticed the effect of being in an overly hot, stuffy and airless room in winter. It can cause drowsiness and inattentiveness.

Artificially introduced scents

Within the home it is important to deal with those smells that breed when things get stale. It can be tempting just to cover them up with stronger smells such as room deodorizers but it is much more useful to address the cause. Clear the rubbish, open the windows, let in the light, wash the clothes — whatever it takes. This will be healthier and less expensive. It makes little sense to be constantly filling the air with highly scented chemicals without dealing with the underlying smells they are being used to mask. Although we don't want to spend our whole life cleaning, regularly dusting surfaces, vacuuming carpets and washing floors help to keep a house smelling fresh. A couple of drops of essential oil on a damp cloth while dusting can simply sweeten and refresh a room.

This is not to say that we might not want to introduce particular scents or perfumes into the environment. If not overdone, they can certainly provide a lovely accent to the atmosphere. These days, however, there are so many products available that we are possibly overdoing the introduction of artificial smells into the environment. For example, there may be separate face, hand and body creams in your bathroom, two different soaps, a shampoo, a perfume, a deodorant, toothpaste, an air freshener and a toilet cleaner — each with their own strong aroma and often all used before we have even left the bathroom in the morning. Each scent not only begins to fight with the others, it produces a kind of sensory overload that negates the appreciation of any particular smell.

It's a little like adding too many competing flavours to a recipe. The best chefs keep things simple and clear so that the flavours are distinct and have space to shine. Similarly, it can be helpful to take this approach with the palate of smells we introduce into our home environment. Lovers of wine might also have noted that if someone wearing a liberally applied perfume or aftershave enters a room while you are trying to smell and savour a wine, that scent will overcome and dominate the ability to fully enjoy the wine.

If using artificially introduced scents, as a general rule it is far healthier to use naturally produced scents like essential oils rather than artificially produced ones that have a range of chemicals in them. Oil burners, incense and scented candles can also create a subtle and lovely ambience in the home if used in moderation.

Gardens, fresh flowers and plants

Apart from the visual effect of having plants or flowers in or around your home, their scents and smells can really enrich and enliven us. This comes not just with flowers but also the subtle but sweet smells associated with growing vegetables and herbs. Having them near a window also brings them into the house.

If choosing flowers for the garden, why not make sure they are scented? You might want to choose a range of plants that flower at different times of the year so that for much of the year there is something of interest in the garden.

It can be simple to introduce 'green spaces' to an apartment — even if you feel you weren't born with a 'green thumb' — whether on a balcony, window ledge or a sunlit corner of a room.

Being mindful of our olfactory environment

From a mindfulness perspective, we would do well to take pleasure in the smells that abound in our home and not take them for granted. For example, take the time to smell the cooking aromas. Smell the food before it is eaten. Smell the polished furniture. Smell the perfume or aftershave your partner is wearing. If we take the time to use and awaken the sense of smell it will not only be more enjoyable and interesting but it will tell us much about the world we live in. The sense of smell is often neglected but can be woken up with a little effort. By and large, from an olfactory perspective, it is important to keep our environment fresh, natural and simple.

Taste

Taste has a privileged place among the senses. It is a sense that we seem to be prepared to pay a lot of money to indulge. Think of how many gourmet food stores there are, how many restaurants, how many wineries, cafes and cookbooks ... There is so much about modern life that is dedicated to the sense of taste.

Why does taste hold a place so close to our hearts? Part of the reason is that taste is very important for making eating such an attractive thing to do, and eating is vital for survival. Things that are so intimately linked with survival will be closely related to the brain's pleasure centre, thus compelling us to do the things that help us to survive. If the things that help us to live — like eating and sex — were unpleasant then we would not do them, we would not survive very long and we would be very unhappy for as long as we did survive. Historically, while food was hard to get and we had to expend a lot of energy getting it, there was not much danger of eating in excess of our requirements.

Changing eating and taste patterns

In recent times three important things have happened in relation to food in developed countries: food has become readily available; the energy required to get food has decreased significantly; and food has become much more processed so that much of its nutritional value is refined out and empty calories pumped in. The problem with this arrangement is that it causes the brain's pleasure centre to be overstimulated in such a way that we feel compelled to keep seeking such readily available pleasure — to keep eating — beyond what is healthy or reasonable. This leads on to addiction. Another issue is that when we feel sad or stressed we get short-term relief by stimulating the brain's pleasure centre. So we might eat for comfort, consolation or pleasure but we don't often eat for need or health.

Yet while eating stimulates the brain's pleasure centre, the strange paradox is that poor quality nutrition is a significant risk factor for poor mental health. For example, in Australia the 20 per cent of adolescents with the poorest quality nutrition have nearly twice the risk of depression compared to adolescents with healthy nutritional patterns.[1] Healthy nutrition is therapeutic for mental health because the brain needs the right nutrients to function well and make all the neurotransmitters and hormones it must make to keep us happy.

Mindless eating

Just as with most other things in life, we generally eat on automatic pilot. We rush in, stuff some food down the gullet and rush out again. We sit in front of a plate full of food, only to look down a few minutes later and notice that the plate is empty. Did we really taste any of the food in between? We might be vaguely aware that the food was hot or cold, fatty or sweet, soft or crunchy, but we generally won't have given it much attention.

Is this a problem? Well, yes, perhaps more than we know. Firstly, we don't get the same emotional satisfaction from the food if we are not really tasting it. Secondly, we won't be likely to pick up the body's satiety messages — the body telling us when it has had enough. We might be way out of tune with what our body actually needs and totally unaware of how fatty, sweet or salty the food is that we are eating. We might also be missing out on the other thing that taking time to eat offers: the chance to eat with the family, to connect and enjoy time together in conversation. Even if a family sits at the table together for a meal these days the children, and increasingly the adults, are likely to be on their mobile devices at the same time. Increasingly, the family meal either doesn't happen at all or it is just treated as a 'pit stop' on the way to somewhere else. Sharing a family meal is not just about nourishing the body, it's about the soul. Interestingly, studies suggest

that, from the perspective of child and adolescent wellbeing, the most important time in the day is the evening mealtime.[2]

In mindfulness-based weight management interventions, participants have showed significant improvement in being able to restrain excessive eating, along with decreases in weight, eating disinhibition, binge eating, depression, perceived stress, physical symptoms, negative affect, and markers of inflammation.[3] People developed healthier eating and felt better as they did it. The key to changing eating patterns in a mindful way was not so much a matter of suppressing or trying to control the urge to eat, which is tiring and stressful, but rather in learning to observe the urge with non-attachment and without being controlled by it. Learning 'urge surfing', as it is called, takes a little practice but is useful no matter what lifestyle change we wish to implement.

MINDFULLY 'URGE SURFING'

As you go about your day-to-day life notice the urge to eat when it arises, such as when you pass a cake shop, get home from work, open the fridge, are having the evening meal or when sitting in front of the television at night. If you catch the urge in the moment, you don't need to suppress it, but just notice it. Perhaps you might also notice what is behind it. Is there boredom, a need for comfort, a feeling of habit or some other motivation? Just pause for a moment. Get in touch with the body. See if the body is actually thirsty or hungry. Notice if the mind starts having an internal debate with itself about being 'good' or 'bad', 'I want to' or 'I shouldn't'. There is no need to judge what you are noticing, just stand back and observe. Connect with a slow breath or two.

Then, based on what you have noticed, consciously and positively decide whether to eat. If you eat then do so with attention, taste the food and eat it slowly. If you decide not to eat, then simply engage your attention with whatever it is you decide to do.

MINDFUL EATING

Here is a mindfulness experiment with eating. It is a meditative exercise known as the 'raisin exercise' and was made famous by Jon Kabat-Zinn. The exercise is best done slowly and deliberately; particular attention will be given to the sense of taste, but all the senses will be involved. You will need sultanas, grapes or some other kind of food such as chocolate or fresh fruit. The whole exercise should go for about 5 minutes. Spend as long as you like on each part, and try to experience as fully as you can each of the senses and the act of eating the sultana. You may want to do it alone or as a family.

First, set aside anything that you think you know about this food. Simply let go of any concepts or ideas you have and, as best you can, bring a fresh, curious awareness to it, as if you were eating it for the first time. It might even help to imagine you are from another planet and have never seen this particular food before in your life.

Take the food and hold it in the palm of your hand, or between your finger and thumb. Pay attention to seeing it. Look at it carefully, as if you have never seen such a thing before. Turn it over between your fingers, exploring its texture ... noticing the edges and how they catch the light ... noticing its shape, and whether the light can pass through it or not. Notice the colour/s. And if any thoughts come to mind like 'What is the point of this?' or 'I don't like this food', then just note these as thoughts and bring your awareness back to the object.

And now smell the object, taking it and holding it under your nose. Notice what happens in your mind as you do this. If you notice any associations or memories, just acknowledge these and then come back to the actual smell of the object.

And now take another look at it ... consciously make the decision to, in a moment, place the object in your mouth. Tune into your body and notice what happens as you start to think about doing this. Pay particular attention to your mouth and your stomach. Notice how your body has already connected mentally with the experience of eating this object, and has already started to prepare itself physically. Perhaps you notice saliva being released. And now slowly bring the object to your mouth, noticing how

your hand knows exactly where to put it, without any conscious thought. Then gently place the object in the mouth, noticing how it is 'received', without biting it, just explore the sensations of having it in your mouth. Perhaps notice the automatic pilot of the urge to start chewing — but just sit with this urge for a moment longer, without indulging it, perhaps learning something about how to ride it as you do so. When you are ready, very consciously and deliberately bite into the object and start to chew it. Notice the release of flavour, and see if you can tune in to where on your tongue you taste the tastes. Notice which teeth are doing the chewing. Feel the activation of the jaw muscles and tune right in to the experience of chewing. Notice the urge to swallow coming up and again just sit with this urge without immediately indulging it. Notice the automaticity of swallowing, and perhaps reflect for a moment on how often you would just eat without much conscious awareness.

Then, when you feel ready to swallow, do this with as much awareness as possible. Notice the movement of the tongue and see if you can stay in touch with the object as it moves down your throat and right down into your stomach. Become aware that the object is now becoming part of your body.

Healthy nutrition

If we get habituated to certain tastes — like very fatty, sugary or salty foods — then the brain calibrates itself to expect the same amount of fat, sugar or salt for the food to taste right, otherwise it tastes bland and unsatisfying. However, if we consistently eat less of that basic taste then over a period of time the brain recalibrates itself and the lesser amount of fat, sugar or salt tastes right. The calibration of our taste for foods high in fat, sugar and salt happens early in life, perhaps it even begins in the womb, and is one of the main drivers of the modern obesity, metabolic and chronic illness epidemics. The tendency to overeat and to eat foods of poor nutritional value is one of the primary causes of lifestyle-related illnesses in developed countries. The issue therefore lies in both the quantity and quality of the food we eat. Add to this the tendency to be sedentary and we have the perfect storm.

So what is a 'healthy diet'? As a general rule, if we are more conscious of our food choices, it is useful to enjoy a wide variety of nutritious, whole foods, taking care to eat fresh, unprocessed foods whenever possible. Growing your own food will help with this, and will also help to increase the amount of fruits and vegetables in your diet.

Reducing your intake of red meat and saturated (animal) fats, along with increasing omega-3 in your diet (via oily fish and flaxseeds/linseeds) is also beneficial to health and wellbeing. Physical activity has many benefits, including helping you maintain a healthy weight.

Obviously you won't be eating your meals so slowly and deliberately as this, nor is there a suggestion that you should, but you can take the thread of that attentiveness into your eating and your life in general.

Eating mindfully doesn't mean that food needs to be bland or unenjoyable — quite the opposite. There are so many creative things to do with food but if we eat more mindfully our tastes may change to prefer whole, fresh and nutritious foods. It will be better for us and for the planet. There is also much enjoyment and creativity to be had in the preparation of food, especially when it involves the whole family. Furthermore, if we are mindful we will also enjoy our food more by actually tasting it and will be far more in touch with our body's needs.

PART 3

the five spaces

Space is the fifth element as described in ancient wisdom traditions after air, water, earth and fire. These physical elements were each associated with a particular sense and each sense in turn related to particular aspects of the mind. So we have the physical experience of 'taste' but also the subtle sense of things being 'tasteful'; the physical sense of 'touch' but also the subtle sense of 'being in touch'; the physical sense of 'sight' but also the subtle sense of 'insight'; the physical sense of 'smell' but also the subtle sense of being able to 'smell a rat'; and we have the physical sense of 'hearing' but also the subtle sense of 'really being listened to'. Thus, when we are really mindful and 'come to our senses' we perceive things on a far deeper level than when in our usual state of being on automatic pilot.

This section of the book is not about different rooms of the house as such, but rather considers the concept of space according to those spaces that facilitate different activities in the life of the home. The basic activities people participate in throughout their home have to do with work

and leisure, socializing, resting, storing things
and being outdoors. We would do well to be
conscious of these particular functions when we
design a home, decorate it and organize it. How
we use the space, whether we leave it clear or
cluttered, how it is organized, what surrounds it
and what we put in it, all have significant effects
on how we feel within that space and what we
do while we're in it.

The Leisure Space

Just as trying to separate one side of a coin from the other, it is hard to inquire into leisure without considering work as well. Increasingly in many countries, people are working from home, too — perhaps one or two days a week are spent working from home instead of at the office, or you might run your own business from the spare room. So we will explore how working life is the background to our leisure life and how we need to be able to compartmentalize one from the other physically and/or mentally. If we can do this well, and if we can cultivate a mindful attitude, then we can reduce the burden associated with work and maybe even convert some of it into leisure.

This transformation relates to what is going on in the mental, rather than the physical, space. This chapter will therefore encompass both these areas — the 'leisure space' is as much, if not more, about the mind as it is about your physical environment.

The relationship between leisure and work

Leisure, by definition, is the time we are not working. It implies being free of demands or requirements and having the time to do the things we would do if we could freely choose. But there is a grey zone between work and leisure. If we are lucky, our work can be like leisure time: creative, enjoyable, interesting. We might love our work as a writer or artist, or perhaps our work involves travel; or we are a winemaker, or work on interesting community projects. Equally, our leisure can sometimes feel like work, as anyone will attest who has spent long hours jogging or at the gym, built their own deck or spent a lot of time gardening.

But whatever it is that we do, if we do it with a greater quality of attention then the activity is transformed, taking on more meaning and giving greater fulfillment. So a menial task such as making a cup of tea can be imbued with significance if seen in the right way. The Japanese tea ceremony is a great example of this. If we do something with little attention then it doesn't matter how grand the activity it is, it will be banal and lacking in meaning. We could be the CEO of a major company providing a great service to humankind, but without focused attention we might just be turning up to work and going through the motions.

We have a curious relationship with work and leisure these days. Some people (for example many who are retired or those who are unemployed or under-employed) might feel they have too much time on their hands, with hours of the day to fill up while warding off boredom. Others who are working long hours, especially in families where both parents are working full time, find they have too little leisure time.

There are also many people who don't enjoy their work. They may find themselves living from weekend to weekend, annual holiday to annual holiday. We might therefore think of leisure hours as being the time when we 'really live' while the great swathes of work hours in between are just something to be endured or survived. Of course, many people find themselves so exhausted from their working week that there is little energy left for social, active or creative leisure pursuits. The leisure time they do have is spent settling, or perhaps slumping, in front of the television.

So, before considering the leisure space in the home, it might be worthwhile taking some time to explore work first.

Choosing our work mindfully

The kind of work we choose can have a profound effect on our state, on how we feel and what we do when we get home. What would a mindful choice of work look like? Well, have we chosen a job or preferably a career — or even better yet, a calling — that fulfills, extends and interests us? Is it creative? Do we feel that we are not only using but developing our abilities and potential? Do we see the value of what we are doing for both our family and the wider community? Is it of use and service to others? Are we really following our passion? If not, then why not?

It is not necessarily easy to choose a career path that ticks all these boxes. Various factors, such as the economic climate, are outside our control but can profoundly influence career choice. We might therefore find ourselves doing whatever work is available, whether we like it or not. Fair enough — we need to work to live. But are there other issues worthy of consideration? Even if the situation is not ideal, is there a way we can take control over our perception of, or attitude to, the work we do? It is not a matter of how grand the job is. Are we not seeing the real value of what we are doing, or the pleasure given to others by the goods or services we provide? Are we being the best we can be in the position? Is 'I can't find something better to do' really a cover for not taking the initiative to do something more meaningful? Perhaps we have more choice than we realize but we haven't really stopped to look.

It is worth taking some quiet, reflective time to consider some of these questions. It matters, not least because our working day (or night) impacts on how we relate to others at home and how much energy we have left for leisure at home.

Work in the home

Work, for many, is increasingly impacting on leisure time at home, and the border between home and work environments can often become blurred. The rise of modern technology and communications has made this more possible than ever before, which is both a blessing and a curse.

Let's now take a look at some particular work/ home issues, including working from home.

THE MENTAL TRANSITION BETWEEN WORK AND HOME

It's strange that many people spend much of their leisure time thinking about work and much of their work time thinking about leisure. It's as if the mind is always wanting to be somewhere else rather than being where we are in the present moment. This is what it means to be unmindful.

In order for us to be able to mentally separate working life and home life it can be very useful to have a mindful 'comma' before arriving home from work, or before beginning work. Taking a few minutes to properly and consciously transition between these two aspects of our life — work and home — can help us to make the transition more smoothly and be far more engaged and refreshed for what awaits us. This pause might take the form of a few minutes of meditation, a shower, changing clothes or a walk in the park, but making this space really helps us to leave the past where it belongs and to be present to what comes next.

WORRY, THE GREAT MASQUERADER

One of the main things that keeps us preoccupied about work, and less able to engage at home, is worry. Worry often does a great job of masquerading as something useful. For example, much of what we think of as planning, preparation and trying not to forget work-related things, is actually worry pretending to be helpful, which is generally why we give it so much attention.

If we apply the mind purposefully, if it is focused and on-task, then we will be productive but not stressed. If the mind is distracted and churning about work then it is worry in disguise. It will be unproductive and associated with stress, pressure and an inability to switch off. Learn to recognize the difference between these two and you will save an enormous amount of grief.

TAKING WORK HOME

Perhaps we take work home with us and find that much of our time at home is invaded by work. From time to time this might be necessary, but it should be the exception rather than the rule. If it is happening all the time then consider whether you are compulsively cramming your evening with work that is really not that vital. Are you doing it because you are feeding your anxiety about being good enough, or to gain a promotion? Are you working inefficiently during working hours such that you leave things unfinished? Would it be better to go to work a little earlier or leave a little later if it means not taking work home? Are you doing a job that is going to help you to lead a happy and balanced life or is it getting in the way of a happy and balanced life? Of course, if you just love your work so much that it feels like leisure even when you are working then by all means take it home, but even then do consider the impact such a way of life could be having on your relationships.

Working from home

Perhaps it is a good and reasonable option for you to work from home. Perhaps it suits your family or lifestyle, or it is economically preferable for some reason. Or perhaps you run your own business from the garage, study or studio. It is also increasingly the case that many people, while still employed on a full-time basis, conduct some of their working days from home. Fair enough, but take care. You might need to be very conscious of separating the work and living spaces within your home.

If you work from home for some or all of your working hours, it can very beneficial to physically close off the work space so that you can mentally close off from it when you need to. Is your home space constantly reminding you of work? If so, do something about it. Can you, for example, set up your work space in a spare bedroom or study, so that you can close the door on work, both physically and mentally, when your working day is done? Know how to physically and mentally extract yourself from work and learn how to *be* home when you are in the home space you use for living not working.

With the rise of the smart phone, the tablet and a plethora of other technologies and devices we can be on call pretty much 24/7 these days. If you're self-employed this might mean that you don't miss that after-hours inquiry. If used well, such technology can be a great servant, but if used poorly then the same technology turns into a tyrannical master. We can find ourselves answering emails or returning calls at all times of the day or night, particularly if we are in charge of our own business or work as a freelance or contract worker. Over time this can create a mindset that everything is urgent and important even when it is not. It doesn't allow the mind to switch off from work and switch on to home. It doesn't allow us to properly refuel and refresh.

What's the answer? Take control! Find the off button. Keep technology away from places it has no right to be, such as the bedroom or dinner table. Compartmentalize your time. Work mindfully when you work and then leave it alone when it is time to stop. If you don't then pretty soon you will be unproductive and unfulfilled at both home and work. It is also really important to help children to cultivate such disciplines early in life, not so much by your words but by your example.

Shifting our attitude to leisure at home

When is a task work and when is it leisure? That is hard to say, but one aspect of leisure is that it is free of necessity, that we choose to do the activity and that we enjoy it. Hopefully we find it fun and creative.

When we are home, how can we create more leisure time and enjoy it more? One way is to foster more enjoyment in those 'chores' we do on a daily basis. For example, we might need to cook in order to live but if when we are cooking we

are wishing we were somewhere else, then we will
add enormously to the burden associated with the
task. Can we make such work more like leisure?
Yes. To start with, making a task more creative
will help make it more fun. You can, for example,
cook and eat together or try new recipes,
techniques or cuisines. Pay more attention to the
activity itself rather than the habitual thinking we
generally entertain about the activity. The more
we notice and engage with what we are doing,
the more we will learn, the more interesting it
will be, the more easily the time will pass and the
more efficient we will be.

Many a man loves to spend time in his shed.
That's interesting in itself, but the same activity
done in the shed could be experienced as work
or leisure depending on your attitude and level
of engagement. To be open and engaged is an
important part of what it means to be mindful.
Anytime we engage fully and are present with
what we are doing, the space where we are will
be potentially transformed into a leisure space.

Leisure as mental stimulation

The human brain needs stimulation, creativity
and active engagement to keep itself healthy.
Stimulation in the form of worry is not mindful
engagement, but rather what the mind does when
it disengages. Leisure time and how we use it
has a very important impact upon our brain and
mental health.

According to research, people in their mid-seventies who were in the top quarter for engaging in cognitively stimulating activities had brains that more resembled people in their twenties; those in the bottom quarter had brains that resembled people with Alzheimer's Disease even before they had come down with the symptoms.[1] When we are not mindful and engaged, the brain slips into what is called 'default mode' and when we spend a lot of time in this state the brain gets gummed up with amyloid, the protein that leads to Alzheimer's.[2] Mindfulness, on the other hand, stimulates the brain to maintain the brain connections and cells it already has, and to make new ones.[3,4] It also switches off default mode and reconnects attention and memory centres.[5] For this reason it is associated with better cognition and memory as we age.[6]

Mindless leisure activities, where we don't pay attention (such as watching television), are associated with a greater incidence of attention deficit problems in children and roughly a fourfold increase in a lifelong risk of developing Alzheimer's compared to those who enjoy leisure activities predominantly requiring attention, such as reading, playing board games, playing musical instruments and dancing.[7,8,9] The average amount

MINDFUL LEISURE TIME EXPERIMENT 1

As you go about your leisure activities, when you remember, bring awareness to your state of focus, mind and emotion. How mentally engaged are you in what you are doing? What is the effect of that activity on your state? Is there a difference between the effect of very passive leisure activities, such as watching television, and very active ones, such as playing sport or games? If you are multitasking or on social media while engaged in your leisure activities then what is the effect of that? What is the effect of 'unplugging' and engaging more fully?

You might wish to choose a particular leisure activity and make a conscious effort to do it mindfully. What is the effect of this on your experience of that activity, your enjoyment of it, how you feel and your state of mind afterwards?

If you want to, do this exercise with your children and see what they find.

of screen-based leisure time that young people engage in is over 4 hours a day and climbing way beyond what is healthy, especially with the advent of increasing forms of electronic media.[10] The invasion of the bedroom by the screen, particularly the computer screen, has for many children and adolescents had a terrible effect on leisure time. By and large it has negatively impacted on their socialization and the dynamics of the family. It also means that many children are spending time unsupervised when they could be putting themselves at risk. As the bedroom has become the primary focus of leisure time it doesn't do what it is intended to do. For many this means poorer sleep and therefore poor mental health. It is better to keep the bedroom for

what it is designed for and to have a shared space in the house that is for work and study, including housing the computer/s there.

The brain thrives on attention, curiosity and engagement and it wastes away with inattention, disinterest and disengagement. Engagement both with people and with leisure activities is vital in keeping the brain healthy. Active and creative leisure time is for the brain what physical activity is for the body. Virtual experiences are far less useful than real ones. If the amount of screen time is limited in the home then children are significantly more likely to engage in physical activity and reduce their risk of obesity.[11] It's a win–win situation.

Spaces dedicated to leisure

When we think of areas in the home we associate with leisure we generally think of the living room or lounge room but these days leisure has become increasingly synonymous with entertainment. The living room is often dominated by the television, with the whole room framed around the TV screen rather than social interaction. More luxurious homes might also have a home cinema. That's all well and good, but it doesn't take much to sit back and receive the fruits of someone else's creativity rather than cultivate creativity ourselves.

In the days before we had so much entertainment on tap, leisure time required more work or input and had to be spent more creatively — we wrote a letter by hand, handmade our clothes, baked our own biscuits, got out into the garden to tend the vegetable patch, played board games or made our own music. In many ways this required us to be more mindful. Now we have labour-saving devices and buy the things we once might have made; mind you, we have to work long hours to buy those things. These days we are generally more passive in our leisure time and too much passive leisure time is associated with cognitive decline.

So what is the message here? Not that we should never enjoy the 'guilty pleasure' of a little passive leisure time like watching television, but that it should not be what we mostly do with our leisure time. We need to allow time to make things, learn things, do things, interact with people, read, write or paint. Do we have a space in our home that makes it easy for us to do such things? If not, then we will be less likely to do them. Perhaps you want a dedicated craft room or part of the garage for yourself or the family. We probably have one or more spaces in the home that make it easy to slump in front of a screen. Do we really need to do that?

THE MEAL TABLE

One daily activity where leisure and social interaction intersect more than anywhere else is the meal table. Do we have an eating space,

whether it be in the kitchen or a dedicated dining room, which is clear, restful, attractive and easily accessible for the family meal or a meal with friends? If the meal table is covered with the detritus of daily life, or if it is being used for work rather than meals, then it is not likely to be the social hub of which tales are told many years later. Many homes have a dedicated dining room, but equally a kitchen with enough space to fit a generous dining table can be a great way to bring the creation and enjoyment of food closer. In traditional Italian homes, for example, this is common and is one way that the love of food, wine and connectedness come together. Dining al fresco when weather permits is also a lovely way to enjoy great food and company.

CLUTTER-FREE SPACE

To be able to come to rest and engage in a focused way in a leisure space, it helps if that space is both functional and pleasant to be in. It's fine to live in a 'well lived-in' rather than sterile home, but being amongst too much clutter is not going to be restful for mind or body.

One of the great spaces for healthy leisure is a comfortable reading chair with a well-positioned lamp behind it.

MINDFUL LEISURE TIME EXPERIMENT 2

You might like to experiment with an evening or a weekend away from screens, phones, email and social media. What is the effect? Do you notice withdrawal symptoms or signs of addiction or compulsion? What happens if you ride those waves and make the effort to engage more fully with where you are and who you are with?

Leisure is a vital and healthy part of a balanced life. It provides a great opportunity to be creative, productive and mindful. It helps enormously if we create a home environment that is conducive to active leisure time and isn't dominated by passive activities. Also important is cultivating a healthy relationship between the work and home environments so that we make it possible, mentally and physically, to switch off from work and on to home when we need to.

11

The Social Space

Considering how much of our leisure time is spent with others, the social space is closely akin to the leisure space. What are some of the elements that help create an inviting and convivial space for being with others? There are plenty of possibilities, but we think the following factors are worth considering. It should have a peaceful and welcoming ambience; it should be comfortable and good for entertaining; and it should be free of unnecessary distractions.

A peaceful and welcoming ambience

Mindfulness and being at peace are closely related and there are few things better than being at peace in the presence of others. In fact, one of the things we value most about the people we feel closest to is that, when in their presence, they not only help us to feel at ease and comfortable with *them* but also with *ourselves*.

A peaceful ambience starts with the neighbourhood. We may or may not be able to do much about noisy neighbours and the general environment, but then there is the garden. A water feature, moving or still, nearly always creates a lovely ambience. There is not only the reflective surface of the water, but the cooling influence in a hot environment, and the way that the water invites birdlife into the garden. Then there are the plants. There is something natural, renewing and beautiful about being surrounded by green.

Within the home it really begins with the entrance. Take a look at the entrance to your own home. Is there a special feature that welcomes guests when they step in the door, such as objects of beauty like art, pottery or glasswork? Is the lighting soft and warm? Or are you going for something grand, expansive and bright? Do you want an entrance which is clear and minimalist? Whichever way you go, the entrance will say something about you and the mood you invite people into the moment they set foot in the house. Being so familiar (or perhaps that should be complacent) we might not be conscious of first impressions as we enter our own home, but they will influence how we and others feel.

Then we enter the house proper. There is a feng shui principle about not being able to see from the front door straight out the back door. The reasons given for this may or may not be right, but there is something that invites interest, inquiry and exploration when a corner or a turn presents us with an interesting and new perspective. If there is a straight passage through the house, attention and energy are drawn straight out the back door.

The importance of the sense of hearing has already been explored but different auditory environments invite very different kinds of social engagement. The sounds of family life and interactions often create a welcoming and stimulating atmosphere. A dinner party, with the clink of plates, cutlery and glasses and the buzz of engaged conversation, has its own beauty. Sometimes it is lovely to just sit back and take it all in. Then there is the 'music' of friends and family congregating in the kitchen and chatting or pitching in for the food preparation.

There may be other times when we create an environment that is far from what we might call peaceful — for example, when throwing a party. Such an environment encourages one kind of social engagement and one state of attention, associated with excitation. This can have its place and be mindful in its own way, but when things go over the top it doesn't necessarily lead to a higher state of awareness or foster the deepest level of engagement. For that, a quieter kind of ambience will help more and perhaps a softer or more soothing kind of music, or simply ambient sounds. Silence invites a different kind of connection if we have the presence and readiness to sit with it. Just as some people can find loud music difficult and confronting, some people can find silence difficult and confronting. If we are a mindful host then we will be sufficiently in touch with our guests to create an environment they feel comfortable with but that is not unpleasant to ourselves or out of keeping with our own values.

Being comfortable

Comfort is both physical and emotional. Physically, we can have too much comfort or not enough. There is little use in having an uncomfortable home environment — unless we are interested in mindfully increasing our ability to tolerate discomfort — because it is hard to be at ease in our interactions with others if we are not at ease ourselves. So a physical space intended for socializing with others is generally better if it is comfortable, but not too much. A chair or sofa that you can feel at ease with will work fine, whether it's in the living room or around the meal table. You could even sit on cushions on the floor if your hips allow it. Recliners or chaises longues, on the other hand, may be all right for a lazy evening watching television but might be too

A welcoming home invites inquiry and exploration

'comfortable' to create an environment conducive to active interest and engagement with others in meaningful conversation. To overindulge will also take the edge off the quality of the social engagement and will leave a residual apathy and heaviness.

Comfort can also be emotional and psychological, beginning with how we welcome people and make them feel at home in our home. Being

147

settled in ourselves helps others to feel settled within themselves. We also need the right amount of space between people when entertaining: they should not be so close that they feel they are on top of each other, and not so far away that they need to use their mobile phone in order to have a conversation with another guest. Too much space is like spreading the coals of a fire too far apart — it loses its heat too easily. Obviously a large space is good for a large gathering but a more intimate space is often better for really connecting with friends and family.

The decoration of the room also contributes to helping people feel comfortable. If you are lucky enough, an indoor space that opens out or looks onto a lovely and inviting outdoor view works a treat. If space is more limited, a well-placed indoor plant can create a similar kind of ambience. In our home, we generally prefer to keep the curtains open when entertaining at night. It welcomes the world in and doesn't make the room feel closed in or small. Each to their own.

149

Good for entertaining

The main venues for entertaining have traditionally been the lounge or living room, the dining room (or kitchen table) and the outdoor space. For entertaining smaller groups, the living and dining areas are most often used, but for larger groups, if the climate allows, the easy and open flow of an outside space makes a huge difference. Outdoor space not only makes it easier to comfortably accommodate a larger number of people but can provide more options for people to choose where they want to be: somewhere noisier, quieter, warmer, cooler, busier, more private, sitting or standing.

One of the great modern inventions is the bi-fold door, which allows you to open an indoor space to connect it with the outdoors. This can create a great ambience, can dissipate noise, ease the flow of people through your home and increase the capacity of your entertaining space considerably.

Being able to cater for guests is oftentimes a challenge. Some kitchens make it easy and some do not. Many miracles have manifested out of the most meagre kitchens, but generally speaking it is worth considering what your physical and emotional resources can reasonably cope with and then tailoring the dinner or party to suit. You might want to have everything done so that

Free of unnecessary distractions

The endless stream into the modern home of mobile devices has become an ubiquitous part of modern life. One of the least attractive aspects of this is the way it has changed how people relate — or don't relate — when in each other's company. The screen often seems to be the main focus of attention and the people are the distraction. It is one thing to use such media to enhance our ability to connect with others, for example when Skyping someone you couldn't otherwise reach, but it is another to be disengaged from the people right in front of us. In this way we often kid ourselves that we are 'connecting' when in reality our life is being flushed down a screen. It may be worthwhile having a house rule that when with others, and especially when entertaining or sharing a meal, such devices are to be turned off, in silent mode or put away. Other unnecessary distractions while socializing could include the white noise of television or radio, and music so loud that it makes listening to people difficult. Unclutter the space physically, mentally and sensorially to enhance mindful interactions with your family and guests.

your guests do not to have to lift a finger; but if it seems appropriate, a great way of bonding can be to have guests contribute to the meal and its preparation. Cooking together brings people together.

With the greater emphasis on electronic media as entertainment, the home theatre, computer, internet and video games have also been added to the 'bucket list' for homemakers. However if overused or relied upon, such activities don't really invite high-quality interaction between people. Possibly many children these days are only comfortable with people when they have something to entertain them and feel exposed without a device to rely on. The answer is not to continuously allow children to withdraw to such comfort zones, but to expand their horizons and invite greater direct interaction with people. The most mindful parents we know have all encouraged and helped their children to converse comfortably with adults, even from an early age. Adults and children are both enriched and enlivened by the interaction.

12

The Quiet Space

This space, possibly more than any other, goes right to the heart of the mindful home. The cornerstone of living mindfully is to carve out time in our day to practise meditation, but in order to make space for it in our day we need a space for it in our home. However, the quiet space in the mindful home is not just about meditation. Whether or not we meditate, our whole home could be a peaceful space where we, and others, find it easy to be quiet and refresh after a demanding day. In this chapter we will address both these aspects of the quiet space.

Room to meditate

Ultimately it is useful and desirable to be able to practise mindfulness meditation anywhere, whether it's on a meditation cushion in a Zen monastery, outside an interview or exam room, or in an airport boarding lounge. At home we might need to learn to meditate even while our son is practising drums, our daughter is on the phone in the next room, or our next-door neighbour is using an orbital sander.

Being able to be present, non-reactive and at peace in all manner of environments is a far greater indication of mindfulness than being only able to have that 'special experience' in a cloistered environment. In fact, the challenging environments can be welcomed as they often provide the best opportunities for developing the equanimity that comes with being mindful. So, in a manner of speaking, the whole world is potentially a meditation space.

Be still in the midst of activity
and vibrantly alive in repose INDIRA GANDHI

However, having a quieter meditation space does have its advantages. We don't have a dedicated room but we have some chairs in our living room where we can enjoy the early morning and evening sun. If using a seat for meditation, it helps if it has an upright back.

Some homes may have the luxury of a room that is particularly dedicated to meditation and other quiet, contemplative pursuits. If so, or even if you nominate part of a room for meditation, then there are some things that will contribute to making that room supportive of meditation. In fact, the meditation space doesn't have to be inside; if the weather and environment are suitable you might prefer to meditate outside in a particular spot in the garden. If you have a space that is dedicated to meditation there are some things that might be worth considering.

YOUR INTENTION

Holding your intention in mind will help you set up the room in such a way that enriches you and makes meditation easier. What is it you want from mindfulness and how are you going to create an environment that will work towards that end? It may be spiritual, it may be wellbeing, it may be pragmatic — it doesn't matter. It's up to you. Wherever you want to point the mind, then hold that in mind when making your meditation space.

WHICH ROOM TO CHOOSE

Preferably you should choose a room where you can have some privacy, which might mean it is necessary to meditate in the bedroom but this isn't the optimal choice. A room associated with sleep, work or entertainment may not make it easy for the mind to either stay awake or settle into meditation.

THE OUTLOOK

Having a room that looks out to a view, green space or water can be very conducive to meditation and quieter pursuits. If the outlook is not naturally beautiful then you can decorate the room or external space in such a way to make it greener or more beautiful.

CARE OF THE ROOM

Keeping your meditation space neat and clean helps you settle and is also in keeping with the whole point of meditation. If possible, natural light and fresh air also help. On a subtle level, outside of meditation time it helps if you are able to preserve the room from activities that are unsympathetic to meditation, such as work and television.

DECORATION OF THE ROOM

The room doesn't have to be empty of furnishings or decoration (although it could be) but it certainly helps if it is not cluttered. Physical spaciousness helps to foster spaciousness of mind. Lighter colours will generally work well, as will curtains that will let in light even when closed. Wallpaper may be used especially if aesthetically pleasing and of symbolic interest, but perhaps not too dark or overly decorated.

FURNISHINGS

Not much is needed. A surface to meditate on is most essential whether you feel comfortable with a mat, cushion, a meditation stool or a chair. Other things might be included such as a table, one or two carefully chosen works of art, a sculpture, a book or two, flowers and a lamp. It helps if the things within the room are sympathetic to, and even symbolic of, the aim of meditation. You won't need a television, mobile phone or other paraphernalia.

THE SENSORY ENVIRONMENT

Gentle lighting such as lamps or even candles work well; too bright an environment can be invasive and too dark can be sleepy. You don't necessarily need them, but if using incense, essential oils or other fragrances it helps if they are not too strong or stimulating, and special care should be taken if the room is a small space with windows closed. In terms of sound, quiet works well, but if the windows are open then ambient sounds are welcomed. You can also use meditative-type music if you wish to practise in that way.

TIMING

Meditation can help us to tune ourselves in to the natural rhythms of the day. Sunrise and sunset are the most conducive times for meditation. In the morning the sunlight is particularly awakening, but if the sun is strong then some shading or dappled light works best. In the evening the energy of the day naturally subsides. As a general rule, it is better to meditate before rather than after food, because food can make us sleepy.

OUTSIDE

If you have chosen outside as your meditation space, say the garden or deck, then many of the abovementioned points still apply — intention, avoid clutter, light, keep the space clean etc.

A place to be

Mindfulness is not reserved only for that time when we are practising meditation. That is where mindfulness starts, but it's what we do when we get out of the chair that really matters.

Anywhere, any time, the home is potentially a quiet space. Living in a more mindful home doesn't necessarily mean we have to turn it into a Cistercian monastery. If we want to live like a recluse then we had better pack our bags, set off to the hills and take our vows (for those entertaining that possibility then the movie *Into Great Silence* might be worth a look). But the so-called 'householder' lives and works in the world. What we can do as a householder is to take the flavour of contemplative life and season our home life with it.

While it is great to enjoy music, watch some television, have conversations, use electrical appliances and the rest, it is also good to avoid excessive noise and to have times in the day free of sound and activity. This gives us time to rest — consciously. Resting consciously is different to resting unconsciously: one is mindfulness and the other is sleep.

Resting consciously doesn't just mean meditation. It also means having some quiet time for more restful pursuits such as reading, craft or creative activities. If you are going to be reading or creating then be mindful in selecting what to read or create. Read something that is nourishing and will make you wiser at the end of having read it. Pursue a craft or creative endeavour that will make the world a more beautiful place at the end of having created it. We should take time for such pursuits on a regular basis. If we don't make the conscious effort to schedule them into our day or week or year, they will constantly be squeezed out by ongoing activity, some of which is productive and necessary but much of which is meaningless busyness and an inability to stop. As one teacher remarked after her first experience of mindfulness meditation: 'I felt so guilty just sitting here and doing nothing'. Mindfulness uncovers what is commonly not obvious to us — an incessant addiction to busyness and the fear of being in our own presence.

Furthermore, the simple activities of daily life — like having a shower, shaving, cooking or washing the dishes — can also be 'quiet time' if they are done mindfully. You see, quiet is not just a physical state. Inner quietness involves the mind being attentive and not off with its distracted incessant chatter. As anyone who has even dipped their toe into mindfulness can attest, we can be outwardly quiet but inwardly experiencing a riot. Equally, we can be outwardly active but inwardly quiet.

Resting consciously is different to resting unconsciously: one is mindfulness and the other is sleep

The gentle sounds of daily life have their own beauty about them. We will hear the difference, if we listen, between a person attentively putting away the dishes and one doing it without attention. In the first case there is the gentle clink of cups and cutlery as they are being put away with care, and in the second there is smashing and crashing. In the first case the person is just in the moment, attending to each action as it takes place, while in the second the person is mentally already impatient or preoccupied about what may or may not be coming next. The number of chips off the rims of plates and cups is one way to measure that!

It is a very helpful practice to put a little space, whether it is a few seconds or a minute or two, between the completion of one activity and the commencement of another. This can make it so much easier to be inwardly quiet and outwardly attentive and efficient as we go about our daily life. If we are patient with this practice and combine it with attentiveness in our daily life then our home will be a more peaceful place for ourselves and for those who visit. It will become a quiet space, a place to be, just be.

13

The Storage Space

One of the common assumptions about meditation in general, and mindfulness in particular, is that we are both able to and should 'empty the mind'. This has led many a mindful aspirant to give up in despair after hours of beating themselves up, because the mind will just not empty itself.

The trick is to use the mind consciously or mindfully — that is, wisely. We need to cultivate the ability to discern between those occasional thoughts that are both relevant and useful — such as a moment of insight into a problem you were working on or remembering that tonight is the night to put out the rubbish — and those that are irrelevant and purposeless. The mind also has the capacity to store things. We call it memory. There are things that are worth remembering like our PIN and phone numbers, or our partner's name or birthday, where we work or where we put our car keys. It may also be nice to remember the holiday we went on last summer, or helpful to remember the mistake we made when learning how to make a bearnaise sauce. But on top of this there is a whole lot of clutter in the mind that has no discernable use despite the fact that it appears to be useful.

Worry masquerades as many things, such as trying not to forget things, or planning and preparation, or trying to work ourselves out.

There is a discernable difference between mindful remembering, planning, preparing and reflecting and unmindful worry. We will feel and function differently. One we need to take note of and make space for; the other we need to leave alone and clear out. If we don't clear out the useless stuff in the mind then there will not be space for the useful stuff.

The home is like the mind

In many ways the home is like the mind. It's where we live. There are useful things in the home that need to be easily accessible from their place of storage. There are other things that have no discernable use, or have outlived their usefulness, and need to be either given to someone who can make use of them or recycled and made into something else which is useful. To hold onto things that are no longer useful, and are not beautiful, leads to clutter. At its worst this is called hoarding and can lead to the whole home environment becoming unsafe, unclean and unusable.

165

Discerning what needs to be kept and what doesn't

When considering storage space, we first need to discern what needs to be retained and stored and what doesn't. Learning to use the mind well is much about discerning between which thoughts are worth giving attention to and which ones are not. It is similar with the home; it is a sifting process that needs discernment. Do we really need all those clothes, all those cosmetic products, all those kitchen implements, all those books, all those plants in pots or all those trinkets? If not, then why are we holding onto them?

Socrates was famous for his austerity, with just an old toga to call his own. Despite this he was content and lacked nothing. Obviously we need the basic necessities of life, but over and above that the gap between what we have and what we desire can be an indicator of the level to which we are unsatisfied. The wider the gap the more we will be in want. The solution of the consumerist society is to acquire more, which puts us on a treadmill that can be hard to get off. The solution suggested by various wisdom traditions is to want less. Now we don't have to live quite as austere a life as Socrates, but it would be worth considering one of his famous maxims: 'How much can I do without?' 'Need' and 'want' can be poles apart.

MINDFUL SORTING

Select an area of the house you need to sort out. Then practise a brief period of mindfulness meditation before you begin — it might just make the letting-go process a little easier. Give yourself a time limit, even 10 minutes, and simply make a start. Be quiet and objective about each item's usefulness and be prepared to relinquish it.

Helping our possessions find their rightful home

Many a home has sufficient storage space but the items don't seem to be able to find their way to it. Why? Is it due to laziness, that we just can't summon the energy to put things away? Have they been lying around for so long that we just don't see them anymore? Are we procrastinating because we think the task has become so great that it is now beyond us?

Well, to quote Shakespeare, 'stiffen the sinews, summon up the blood'. Take some mindful time to stop, connect with the senses and be awake to what is in front of you. If you feel you are too busy to deal with finding a place for each item, then take a few mindful moments and gently but deliberately start by giving attention to just one small part of the larger task.

In the majority of homes there is enough space to house the things we *need*, but not for all the things we want or cling to. If we want less and cling less, we can then put away the things that we do have a use for. It's amazing the effect this has when we actually do it. You will feel mentally clearer and refreshed. The external space will reflect your internal space. There is space again, you can move again, and you can find things you need again. It's just like that in our mindful moments: yes, there are thoughts in the mind

that we can draw on when we need them, but we don't have to be churning through all of them all of the time. As thoughts present themselves to us in daily life be aware and engage with the ones that are relevant and leave the ones that are not. They will put themselves away if we let them.

Storing things in the home

There are plenty of books and companies dedicated to storage solutions in the home. Some very smart and creative people have given some quality attention to finding better ways to store things in the kitchen, wardrobe, shed, laundry, cellar and every other nook and cranny within the home. Our hats go off to these problem-solvers of modern domestic life.

There are five main elements to an effective storage space. The more of these boxes we can tick the better. To be most effective, a storage space:

- **makes efficient use of available space within the home**

- **stores more things in a given space**

- **stores items securely and safely**

- **makes stored items more accessible when they are needed**

- **is as aesthetically pleasing as possible.**

When well thought out, storage solutions can be as beautiful as they are functional. We will not even attempt to list and describe all such storage possibilities, but getting some advice from an expert, or a friend who has made use of such creative ideas is a good place to start.

14

The Outdoor Space

The outdoor space varies enormously from one home to the next. You might live in a rural or remote area with a paddock, mountain or desert as your backyard. Then there is the traditional suburban block with a house and front and back gardens. More recently the suburban block has come to accommodate a very large house pressed to the boundaries and a much smaller garden. There is the small inner city block, the subdivided block and the unit or apartment with a small courtyard garden. Increasingly these days there is the high-rise apartment with or without a balcony as the outdoor space. No matter which way we go, there is something important about connecting to the outdoor space at home.

*It is a basic human
need to connect with
nature and the outdoors.*

The importance of the outdoors

Stepping outside helps to make and keep us
mindful. It enlivens the senses. Fresh air and
natural light, the vagaries of the weather and
ambient sounds and smells all have a way
of awakening us from the slumber-inducing,
hermetically sealed indoor world in which many
of us live and work. Particularly in cities, living
and working in climate-controlled environments,
where the windows are often sealed and the light
is artificial, has a way of disconnecting us from
the elements and from nature. It's almost as if
we forget they exist, and if we don't know about
something, if we ignore it or cease to care about
it, then it is easy to abuse it. Perhaps this is one
of the main causes of the environmental crisis we
now confront.

175

One of the other reasons we place less value on outdoor time at home is that, with the rushed and time-poor modern life we generally lead, gardens are often seen as too demanding on our time and resources — a luxury we have neither the time nor energy to look after. Furthermore, the more screen-based leisure time we have the less likely we are to get outside or be physically active.

Whether we recognize it or not, it is a basic human need to connect with nature and the outdoors. Our brains and bodies have evolved to need the outdoors. On a physical level, if we don't get even a small amount of time in the sun on a regular basis we will find it hard to maintain a healthy vitamin D level. Reconnecting with the outdoors is a great way to become more physically active and therefore more healthy and happy.

Mindfully shaping your outdoor space

There are a number of ways we can shape and connect better with the outdoors at home, even if we don't have that suburban block or generous garden. The simplest way to start is to bring the

AN OUTDOOR MINDFULNESS EXERCISE

Sit in your outdoor space, take some time to come into the present moment and see what presents itself to you. What is in your outdoor space? How does it make you feel? What is not there? Is anything needed to enrich it aesthetically or functionally? How can you create a space that you and your visitors can enjoy and want to be in?

outdoors inside by opening the windows or doors where possible. At the same time as we invite the outdoor space to come inside we will also be improving the air quality of the indoor space.

Following are some more suggestions to help you more mindfully enjoy the outdoors when at home.

SMALL SPACES

When considered and planned mindfully, small spaces can provide an inviting and uplifting outdoor area. Even if you only have a balcony, you can make a very attractive 'green space' by introducing flowering plants, herbs or compact fruit trees. Apart from the appealing ambience that green provides, you will be drawn outside by the need to care for the plants.

THE INTERACTION BETWEEN OUTDOORS AND INDOORS

Consider how you think of and interact with the outdoors while indoors. For example, create an interesting outlook that you can enjoy from where you sit inside. Consider where to place a plant, statue, shed, gazebo or water feature so that you gain maximum enjoyment while still inside your home. In this way you can still maintain a connection with the outdoors, and still feel its presence, when inside.

CARE FOR YOUR OUTDOOR SPACE

Make the outdoor space of your home usable and pleasant to be in. Avoid clutter and have somewhere pleasant to sit and something comfortable to sit on, especially if the available space is a compact or courtyard garden. Use the space well and care for it so that you feel drawn to go out into it rather than repelled by it. Introducing interesting sculptures or a water feature will further entice you outdoors, and inviting the birds in by providing a bird bath or

Think beyond the boundaries and explore your neighbourhood

bird feeder will encourage greater contact with nature. It's also important to ensure you provide yourself and others with shade from the sun, especially in hotter climates.

GARDENING FOR PRODUCTION AND PLEASURE

Enjoy the simple pleasure and sensory experience of getting your hands dirty. Feel the earth and connect with it. Grow things in it. Make your outdoor space productive by planting herbs, fruits and vegetables. The more you connect with

it the more you will realize that there are miracles taking place every day as nature turns soil, light, air and water into things that are beautiful or that we can eat.

CREATIVITY AND WORK OUTDOORS

Be creative with the outdoors. Where feasible, design and do the outdoor landscaping work yourself. Build your own deck. Shape the garden beds. Pave your own paths. Choose the plants and plant them yourself. Make it interesting and

let it reflect something about you. By all means get some advice or professional help if needed, but making a personal investment in the outdoor space you live in will be an ongoing source of creativity and satisfaction. It counters the non-active office work that many people do in their working day.

In designing or renovating your outdoor space, keep in mind the climate and the amount of time you have available to maintain the space. Ignoring these can mean either the garden suffers by being wrong for the climate you live in, or you suffer by trying to maintain a high-maintenance garden when you don't have the time to do so.

If you do need to work in your outdoor space, then do it mindfully. Avoid, if you can, the tendency to have your attention on an internal dialogue about how onerous the work is. Connect your attention with the senses as you work — touch, smell, sight, hearing and, if appropriate, taste.

ENTERTAIN OUTDOORS

When weather and space permit, entertain outdoors. There is something enriching about going al fresco. The food seems to taste so much better! With the right furniture and shading it will be pleasant and great fun.

THINK BEYOND THE BOUNDARIES

Know the outdoor spaces in your neighbourhood. Investigate the bike and walking paths, the waterways and parks. Get out and walk amongst it. Apart from the benefits of exercise, you will meet more neighbours and develop a much greater sense of community. If you have a dog, then take the opportunity to walk it around your neighbourhood; having a dog is a great way to get people outside.

PART 4

home as a healthy environment

Living consciously is a win—win situation. It is enjoyable, much more so than living on automatic pilot, plugged in to a device but unplugged from the environment we live in. Living consciously is also healthy, not only for us personally but also for the planet we live on. We can't make healthy choices in our life unless we have a basic level of information and are in tune with the natural laws that govern our physical health and the environment.

So the last section of the book will explore issues relating to home being a healthy environment. Building biologist Narelle McDonald took the lead in writing 'A healthier home', which looks at how we can help to keep our home free of unnecessary or excessive exposure to the chemicals and pollutants that are so ubiquitous these days. 'A sustainable home' explores how we can reduce the home's environmental footprint and use energy and resources more efficiently. But environment is not just about chemicals, water, energy and air.

It is also about living a measured life, about our own health and wellbeing, and about people, place and community. So the last chapter, 'A measured life', will give a brief overview of how to mindfully care for our physical health, as well as exploring the social environment and how we engage with the neighbourhood and wider community.

A Healthier Home

with Narelle McDonald

As with maintaining a healthy body, maintaining a healthy home requires preventative steps. There are many elements in a building that can affect your quality of life, your physical health and your emotional wellbeing. Our homes are living organisms; indeed, building biologists refer to them as our third skin. In feng shui, homes are considered a reflection of ourselves. This holistic approach encourages us to be conscious of the choices we make in regards to our environment on a daily basis. A healthier home means a happier life. Together in this chapter we will explore how to begin consciously creating a healthy home and how to make better consumer choices. We will discuss the bad news first, in terms of some of the things at home that can negatively impact upon health; then we will discuss the good news in terms of what to do about it.

Effectively I had been living in a tightly sealed toxic soup of chemicals. At that time, not once did I consider that my symptoms might be related to my home. It is hard to know exactly how much the home environment contributed to my ill health, but had I the knowledge I now have I would have made different choices, which would probably have saved me a whole lot of time and money.

Investing in our health in all aspects of our life is important because everything is interconnected. We all know that we need to eat and sleep well, exercise, invest in quality health care and practise mindfulness, but we also need to be conscious of our environment. Our bedrooms are particularly important given that we spend, on average, 22 years of our life sleeping in them. The right choices in the products we use on ourselves and in our homes can either enhance our health or inhibit it.

An important element in creating a healthy home is recognizing that just because a product is common doesn't necessarily mean it's safe. There is often a misconception that if it's on a supermarket shelf it's been thoroughly tested. That, however, is not the reality. Manufacturers don't have to prove a product is safe, it is up to us to prove a product is harmful.

We are where we live

We are intimately connected to our homes, and everything we do in them can have an impact. When I lived in London years ago the flat I chose to live in affected my health immensely. It was a brand new, tightly sealed apartment on the first floor of a big block. It was tiny and contained wall-to-wall synthetic carpets, even in the bathroom. The cabinetry was all particleboard, the kitchen floor was a PVC linoleum and the furnishings were all brand new, including the mattress and sofas. Within weeks of moving in I developed chronic respiratory and sinus issues that doctors were at a loss to treat. The symptoms didn't clear up until we moved out.

The greatest wealth is health. VIRGIL

Part of living mindfully at home is making conscious and discerning choices for the wellbeing of ourselves, our family and our planet. In the words of well-known environmentalist David Suzuki, 'Our personal consumer choices have ecological, social and spiritual consequences. It is time to re-examine some of our deeply held notions that underlie our lifestyles.'

Why is a healthy home so important?

Current health statistics show alarming rises in many allergies, learning disorders and other chronic illnesses. Allergies and autoimmune diseases are amongst the fastest growing chronic conditions in developed countries.[1,2] For example, a peanut-free school was unknown in the 1970s yet peanut allergies have doubled in just the last 5 years, while hospital admissions for anaphylaxis have increased fourfold in the last 20 years.[3] We have to ask what has changed so much in the last 40 years that has made our children so uniquely susceptible to allergies. These statistics show us why this is such an incredibly important subject to bring awareness to.

CHEMICAL EXPOSURE

There is probably a range of factors contributing to the modern population being so allergy-prone, but one important factor that is generally ignored could be the total chemical load we are subjected to. In developed countries today, there are over 80,000 chemicals in widespread use, most of which have not been fully tested for their impacts on human health.

When we take into account the huge amount of chemical exposure that is part and parcel of modern life, a picture starts to develop. How can we keep exposing ourselves and our children to toxins without expecting it to have an impact? It is our children that are particularly vulnerable as they are very susceptible to their environments and the pollutants within them. Their immune systems are immature and still developing, and

189

they have higher metabolic rates, meaning they breathe more air. They are also closer to the floor, drink more water and eat more food relative to their body weight.[4] Incredibly, toddlers can put things in their mouths up to 76 times per hour and may ingest up to 2 teaspoons of dust per day.

Often you will be able to initially smell the chemical components that are giving off gases in your home, such as the smell of new carpet and new paint. Over time we become used to these smells and no longer notice them; however, this does not mean they may not still be there and having an impact on us. Volatile organic compounds (VOCs) are found in a range of products, such as paints, adhesives, fabrics and wood preservatives and become airborne at room temperature. Common symptoms from exposure to such compounds can include eye, nose and throat irritation, nausea, coughing, confusion, fatigue, dizziness and memory impairment.[5]

Formaldehyde is found in manufactured wood products such as particleboard, plywood and MDF. This is a known carcinogen and is banned in some countries but is extensively used throughout modern buildings in others. It can also be found in other unexpected items such as mattresses, clothes, sheets and anything that is listed as crease resistant or wrinkle free. Other widely used compounds that are a part of many artificial fertilizers, insecticides and herbicides can have negative effects on the body's hormonal regulation and alter gene expression. These are called endocrine disrupting chemicals (EDCs). These are just a few examples of what we may be exposed to, and this is not even scratching the tip of the iceberg.

For such a long time we have been programmed to believe that we need an arsenal of cleaning products to make our homes a safe environment for our families. If we backtrack to our grandparents' era they did not treat their homes the way we treat ours today. Our products have changed and what we are cleaning with, bathing with and lathering ourselves in are synthetic chemicals, most of which are not necessary.

ELECTROMAGNETIC FIELDS

Electricity is an important and beneficial part of our daily lives. Our modern world today bears little resemblance even to our grandparents' world, so immense have been the changes since World War II. There is now practically nowhere that is not affected by the signals that we humans have been progressively adding.

Our children are exposed, from the womb, to multiple sources of radiation on a continual basis unlike anything previous generations have encountered. Excessive exposure to electromagnetic fields, such as living close to high-voltage power lines, is associated with a range of health problems, including leukaemia, particularly in the young.

Appliances such as microwave ovens, hair dryers and electric blankets do not seem to be associated with an increased risk of cancer or other significant illness. Although there are electromagnetic fields involved with their use, the level is probably low enough that it is not a major health concern. However, some groups, such as the BioInitiative Group — an international collective of scientists and researchers — are more concerned, particularly for children, and have called for new health safety limits.

Should we panic? No. Should we take care? Yes. By having a simple understanding of this type of hazard we can take steps to minimize our exposure to electromagnetic fields.

INDOOR AIR QUALITY

Today we spend over 90 per cent of our time indoors. In recent decades significant changes have been introduced into the way we build houses — mass-produced materials have been introduced that, along with tighter building envelopes and a lack of fresh air exchange, have contributed to 'sick building syndrome'

Let your home breathe

and the unhealthy buildings of today. Indeed, the US Environmental Protection Agency has ranked indoor air pollution as one of the top five environmental risks to public health. Our buildings have also increased in size and thereby use much more energy to heat and cool.

There are, however, ways to better care for the quality of air in your home, and we will provide some tips in the following section.

A mindful approach to a healthy home

Having described the problem it now makes sense to describe a few simple solutions. We can't always control what we are exposed to out in the wider world but we do have control over our own homes. Creating a healthy home will give us a supportive environment to come back to at the end of the day, allowing us to rest, regenerate and heal. Following are some positive changes you can make to create a healthier home environment.

A HEALTHY BUILDING

Buildings that are connected to nature and have a flow about them can uplift all who live there. The choice of building materials and interior finishes is important not just for the health of your home and yourself but for the planet as well. A healthy home equals a safe home.

So what does a healthy building look like? Firstly, it is a building that has a positive impact on its occupants; it includes an appropriate amount of fresh air, light, thermal, acoustic and spatial comfort; where possible it avoids the use of synthetic materials and toxins; it maintains a connection both to nature and the building's surroundings; and it considers the impact of the building on the entire environment.

AIR QUALITY

There is a number of positive steps we can take to improve the quality of the air in our home. In the first instance it is helpful to use low or, ideally, non-polluting building materials and products that allow the building to breathe. For example, instead of using polyurethane on floorboards, use natural wood oil that allows the timber to breathe. This will in turn help regulate the relative humidity, which then also helps to control dust mites. Old carpets can be significant sources of dust and mites and sometimes it is better to replace them or change to having polished floorboards.

The ideal way to ventilate your home is by using natural ventilation. Open your windows whenever possible to let fresh air circulate throughout your home. Using a vacuum cleaner with a HEPA filter will also help reduce the number of irritants in the air, such as pollens and dust mites. It is also important to ensure all of your exhaust fans are working and vented externally.

OTHER CHANGES

Simple changes such as drinking filtered water and eliminating artificially fragranced products from your home can make a big difference. Adopting even one change can contribute to better health, while several changes can significantly improve quality of life.

Further effective and inexpensive changes that will help you to minimize your everyday exposure levels include: taking your shoes off at the front door; choosing personal care and cleaning products that don't contain harmful chemicals (this includes anything with fragrance); swapping plastics for stainless steel, glass or ceramics.

MINDFUL PURCHASES

Understanding the choices available when purchasing new items gives us the tools and knowledge to make better choices. If you are in the market to buy new furniture or doing renovation work, there are a number of elements to consider.

Part of living mindfully is not just being a consumer operating on automatic pilot and never questioning what we do. We need to be informed and aware of the impact our choices have on ourselves and also on others. So before making a new purchase for your home, query what it is made of, and where and how the product was made. In terms of looking after the health of you and your family, also ask if the item has been treated to be UV resistant, stain resistant, antibacterial or crease resistant. Note, too, that

imported furniture pieces are often fumigated, so look for locally made items where you can. Also, avoid MDF bedroom furniture; opt instead for natural wood finished in low VOC finishes.

When choosing fabrics for your home, remember that the more natural and untreated a fabric, the better it is for your health. Fabrics such as organic hemp, wool, cotton, linen and latex are all good choices. When painting, opt for plant-based, zero- and low-VOC paints, adhesives and sealants.

To help reduce the electromagnetic fields in your home, install hard-wired connections for the internet instead of WiFi and a demand switch on the power circuit to quieten the whole house at night.

Each new day brings fresh opportunities to explore different options and choices to create a home that will support and nourish you today and in the future. Even the smallest decisions we make can enhance our wellbeing and improve the health of ourselves, our homes and our planet.

For a detailed guide to the types of plastics you might find in your home, and how to recycle them, please visit the website at www.mindfulhome.net

A Sustainable Home

Not so long ago, the environment wouldn't have loomed large as a political or economic issue, but how times have changed. Now it is such a large issue that it is impacting on public policy and international politics in very significant ways. On a personal level, it is easy to overlook the impact our personal day-to-day choices have on the planet as a whole. But we do have an impact.

We are all connected

We are all on this planet together and if things go bad on planet Earth there isn't a plan B. It's as if we're all on the *Titanic*, but it has no engines and we each have an oar. As an individual we can't do much to turn the boat on our own. Yet if a high proportion of individuals ignore their individual responsibility and do not row, the momentum of the boat will see us hitting the iceberg in a not too skillful way. On the other hand, it will only take a majority of individuals to catch on to a mentality that we each need to put our oars in the water and work in a coordinated way, and the boat will start to turn. If we are lucky we might only scrape the iceberg instead of hit it head on.

Well, we all have the chance to put our oar into the water at home.

Barry Commoner was a well-known environmentalist in the middle part of the twentieth century. He outlined a number of environmental precepts, with the first one being: 'The first law of ecology is that everything is related to everything else.' It is easy to forget how interconnected we all are. The elements like air, water, earth and energy are constantly interchanging and mixing. Goodness knows where the atoms that make up our own body were before we ingested them.

Ecological footprint

The concept of an ecological footprint has been around for a while. It is a method of calculating the impact on the environment of an individual, organization or even a country.

A home can take out of the environment a certain amount of resources, such as energy or water, and return another amount to the environment. The overall impact is assessed by calculating the 'area of land and water required on a continuous basis to produce all the resources consumed and assimilate the waste products produced.'[1]

It is possible to calculate the ecological footprint of an object by an 'input/output' analysis. Take, for example, a cotton shirt. Its ecological footprint is made up of both direct and indirect inputs, like the area of land required to grow the cotton, the energy required to harvest it, the energy and resources required to produce the fertilizer and chemicals needed to grow the cotton, as well as the water required. A similar calculation can be made for any household item, and indeed for the household overall. In the end a figure is calculated as to how much land would be needed to keep a person living in the manner to which they have become accustomed.

The ecological footprint of a country like Bangladesh is approximately 2.5 acres per person required for sustainability. In Australia and Canada it is about 18.5 to 21 acres per person, while in the United States it is about 30 acres. This is largely because of the amount of food, products and energy people in each country tend to use. Currently the world has about 22 billion acres of productive land, and if that were divided equally between its 7 billion people then there would be about 4 acres per person. Clearly in developed countries we are using a lot more than is sustainable.

Simple is often best

The Triple Bottom Line

The Triple Bottom Line (TBL or 3BL) is another interesting and important concept to help us make decisions of environmental importance. Traditionally, decisions regarding the environment were made primarily with economic interests at heart. The TBL, however, is a way of encouraging people to also bring environmental and social considerations into their decision-making. A good decision needs to be beneficial for all three dimensions — environmental, social and economic — and any decision which negatively impacts upon one will, eventually, negatively impact on the others.

The TBL was originally used by corporations, government institutions and NGOs but is equally relevant for those significant decisions we make at home, for example about where to live, what to purchase or invest in or how to design our home. The three 'bottom lines' are not always stable and sometimes they apparently conflict.

So, an environmentally responsible investment does not always make the most profit, at least not in the short term, but if we have a long-term view we may see it as the best investment. Purchasing solar panels for the roof might look to be initially economically costly, and could take years to turn a profit, but we might decide to install them anyway because we want to do our bit to reduce our ecological footprint and the use of fossil fuels.

Practical ways you can care for the environment

There are many different things you can do to make your household more environmentally friendly. In fact, in many ways you can even give back to the environment rather than just take from it. Bringing a mindful awareness to our decisions regarding environmental impact can help us make choices that are better for us, our home and the planet.

PHILOSOPHY

It is easy to unconsciously take on a consumerist attitude to life. However, cultivating an attitude of not consuming more just for the sake of it will be healthy for us and the environment. A mindful approach will be both realistic and simple: realistic in the sense that all living things need to consume to live, but neither too much nor too little is the healthiest path; simple in the sense that if we are more at peace with ourselves we can enjoy the good things of life without being driven by the kind of hankering that often fuels rampant consumerism. In the book, *Affluenza: The all-consuming epidemic*, the authors define affluenza as 'a painful, contagious, socially transmitted condition of overload, debt, anxiety and waste resulting from the dogged pursuit of more.'[2] If you suspect you have a dose of affluenza then please see your local philosopher for an assessment and treatment.

WASTE AND RECYCLING

If we do not recycle the materials we use in our home then sooner or later we will turn the planet into one big rubbish tip. There are a number of simple strategies we can apply to be more proactive in recycling waste materials.

Recycling refers both to waste items, such as old paper and plastic, and to those items which still have life but for which we might no longer have a use. For these items it is important to find a home. One person's rubbish may be another person's treasure. Rather than throw them out you might want to give them to a charity, friend, student or a lover of restoring old things. Or you might want to give a new lease on life to a pre-loved item from someone else. There are even some artists who create artworks solely using recycled materials.

Recycling should also be done in a healthy and safe way. Most homes these days have easy access to recycling bins with trucks collecting waste products such as plastic, paper, glass and metals. These are easy to process for re-use.

There are a number of toxic products used around the home which are harmful to the environment but which must nonetheless be disposed of, so care must be taken when doing so. For example, paints, chemicals, batteries, polystyrene and fluorescent lights need to be delivered to a waste management plant or collected by the council or local authorities for processing. Televisions, computers, printers and mobile (cell) phones also create vast mountains of waste these days and need to be disposed of in an environmentally friendly way.

Check your council or local authority for information about the services provided in your area. There is likely to be a lot more than you realize.

ENERGY EFFICIENCY

Just as we use our personal energy and time efficiently when we are mindful, so too do we use our resources and time efficiently if we are mindful in the home.

There are two main aspects to the energy equation: energy out versus energy in. Firstly, we can reduce the energy going out by conserving our use of it. This requires commitment from not just one member but from all members of the household. The following energy-saving tips can help your household reduce the amount of energy used.

With a mindful attitude to life, we can see that the simplest approach is often best. Therefore, when considering how best to minimize energy used to heat or cool your home, first consider your clothing — dress appropriately for the weather. So before you turn up the thermostat on a cold day, consider adding another layer of clothing. Similarly, in summer ensure you wear light, loose clothing made of natural fabrics that will allow the body to 'breathe'. Another simple measure is to ensure you only heat or cool those rooms in use.

In order to minimize the amount of energy used to maintain a comfortable temperature in your home, you need to consider how best to keep warmth *in* during winter and heat *out* during the summer. Suitable ceiling insulation is one way to do this. Sealing up gaps in walls, floors and ceilings is also effective, as is sealing any external doors with draught stoppers at the bottom and weather stripping around the frames. If you live in a climate where you feel air conditioning is necessary, choose evaporative rather than refrigerative air conditioning. It will use far less power and keep the air fresh inside your home.

Close blinds, curtains, windows and doors on cold days to keep in heat, and let direct sunlight in where possible. In summer, use outside shading to keep direct sun off the windows of your home. Close windows after the early morning on very hot days to keep out warm air. Double-glazing can make a massive difference to energy use for heating and cooling.

While heating and cooling our homes can take considerable energy, there are other areas of energy use to which we can turn our mindful attention. Check the seal on your refrigerator to be sure it is tight and free from gaps. Be sure to turn off at the wall any appliances not in use, such as the television, computers, coffee makers and toasters. Use energy-efficient light globes such as LEDs, and avoid halogen downlights. Wash your clothes using cold water when you can and dry outside on a clothesline or rack.

Compare electricity suppliers to check you are getting the best deal, and choose an energy provider with a strong investment in renewable energy. Other important energy issues include considering the energy efficiency of an appliance before buying it. Seek advice on the way you design or renovate your home to make use of passive solar principles. It may be worthwhile (and a good investment) to have a consultation with an independent expert in sustainable home design, who will be able to assess what is currently there and what is possible with relatively little cost and effort.

Next, we can increase the 'energy in' part of the equation through the energy we produce at home. Electricity and hot water from solar energy is probably the most widely used means to achieve this, but if you are in a rural and remote area then there are other options too, like wind energy. It is easy to calculate how many kilowatts you might need to generate to offset or even eliminate your electricity bills. Generally, it takes just a few years for solar panels to have paid for themselves.

Transport is a big output of energy for most homes. Apart from what has already been mentioned about energy-efficient and clean cars, there are other things to consider. Is car pooling

an option? What about public transport or riding a bike? Is working from home an option? Can we offset air travel emissions? These are all ways to bring a mindful approach to how we use and care for our precious environment.

WATER USAGE

As the climate changes there are many countries in the world having to cope with more extreme conditions such as flooding, while others are coping with more frequent droughts. Our attitude to water has also largely changed, from viewing it wastefully in the past as an infinite resource, to a more frugal approach today. The way water is used in the home has changed enormously in recent years, particularly in dry climates. Shorter showers, turning off the tap while brushing teeth, not hosing down the driveway, and using a bucket rather than a hose to wash the car are all examples of a more conscious and intelligent use of water in the home.

There are many simple measures for further improving water usage at home. Installing water-efficient showerheads and low-flow taps can greatly reduce the amount of water you use daily, as can installing dual-flush toilets and using a front-loading clothes washing machine.

The garden is also a very important part of the water usage story in many dry-climate households. The impact can be reduced by doing simple things such as using grey water on the garden (take care with the detergents and soaps you use, and note that grey water should not be used on any fruits, vegetables or herbs you are planning to eat). Install a water tank and use the water it collects for the garden or toilet flushing. Watering the garden early in the morning or in the evening, watering the roots rather than the leaves, using mulch and choosing plants that cope well with heat and dry conditions can also help enormously.

FOOD AND PRODUCE

We mentioned earlier that a good rule to follow is to ensure everything in your home is either beautiful or useful. The same principle applies in the garden. Beautiful plants enrich us emotionally and edible plants enrich us physically. And many plants are both beautiful and edible.

Not everyone will have the space, time or inclination to produce food at home, but it is great if we can. It brings us back into connection with the soil, sun and cycles of the seasons. There are few things better than harvesting fresh fruit, vegetables and herbs from your own garden. You know exactly where they have come from, how they were grown, the chemicals they were exposed to (hopefully none) and the distance from paddock to plate is measured in footsteps not thousands of miles. Even balcony gardens

can produce food; there are compact fruit trees that have been developed to make it possible for just about anyone to be a link in their own food chain.

In our home we haven't tried to turn the garden into a mini farm, but we have productive plants and fruiting trees all around the yard — plum, lemon, feijoa, mandarin, orange, Tahitian lime, kaffir lime, two cumquat trees, blackcurrant, persimmon, nectarine, apple, grape and two olive trees. There is also a small but productive vegetable patch and herb garden. We appreciate not just the food that comes from our little block of land, but also the simple joy of seeing nature work its miracle of turning dirt, water, compost and sunlight into something fresh, delicious and nutritious.

Beautiful plants enrich us emotionally;
edible plants enrich us physically.

Preparing food — not just cooking meals, but taking primary produce and turning it into something else — is another consideration for the sustainable home. This includes baking the bread, making the jams and jellies, preserving the lemons, bottling the olives, grinding the spices, producing the dips and making the cheese, etc. Admittedly many people don't have time to do all of this but it is such a sensorial and satisfying thing when we can. It can be great fun and educational for children as well.

For many people, modern living has created a sense of being removed from the environment. Many children may never get outdoors into the garden. It is a tremendous education for children to take part in helping something grow in the garden, to pick it and to make it into something creative. That's connection and that's education.

Another thing to consider with regard to food is being an environmentally conscious consumer. You might want to lower your meat intake and increase plant-based foods in the diet. This is not only healthier for you but it is far less environmentally demanding. Organic produce will be grown in a way that is kinder to the environment and requires far fewer toxic pesticides, herbicides and fungicides. Prefer foods that are local and in season, because they require less energy for production and transport. These are just a few ideas for the sustainable consumer.

PRODUCT CHOICE

We have an important responsibility when choosing products to select those that create the smallest ecological footprint. Approach new purchases mindfully, and first ask yourself if the item is necessary. If you decide that it is, then where possible opt for items in line with principles of caring for the environment. Aim to choose, for example, a car that is fuel efficient and low polluting, or timber products and

furniture harvested from sustainable forests. Buy foods that are produced in ethical and environmentally sustainable ways, ensure you purchase household cleaning products that are environmentally friendly, and check that building products you plan to use are the least toxic available. And if you can afford it, invest in products that will have a long life as opposed to inbuilt obsolescence. Also, try to invest in companies that are conscious of their social and environmental responsibilities rather than just their economic ones.

When purchasing something, keep in the back of your mind that if it doesn't pass the sustainability test it should probably not be purchased. Look at another brand that does.

The (triple) bottom line is, there is a lot we can do to make our home more environmentally friendly. It requires a bit of energy and attention but the payoff is a healthier, safer and more economical home. There isn't a downside, so there isn't a good reason not to do it. Then, in the process of caring for those we live with, we will be simultaneously caring for the planet — our big home.

A Measured Life

In common usage we think of the word meditation meaning things like contemplation, thought or reflection. But one of the more interesting etymologies, according to the *Oxford Dictionary*, is that meditation is actually derived from a word meaning 'measure' and is related to 'mete', as in 'to mete out' or to measure out something. The correlation isn't obvious, so what might this mean? Here is one possibility. Perhaps meditation, when it relates to drawing attention within, takes us to that immeasurable, unlimited and indefinable aspect of our being or consciousness. When it relates to focusing the attention outwardly, it helps us to live and work with attention and precision, that is, in a measured and effective way. It is hard to say, but living our daily life healthily, happily and effectively most definitely requires attention and a measured approach.

Measuring the day, the life

What does it mean to have 'a measured life' or to 'measure the day'? In keeping with the theme of this book it means to pay attention, and through attention to do anything no more and no less than time, place and situation require.

There are various options we can follow in terms of living our life. We can, for example, be formulaic in the sense of having a recipe or plan. So we could follow lifestyle advice telling us how much exercise to do, what to eat and when, how much to sleep, how much to meditate, how often to work and so on. This is useful especially if it is based on some reasonable evidence. Such a plan, schedule or set of disciplines can be a great remedy for a life that is way out of balance or undisciplined to the point where we are suffering significant problems as a result. Like having someone navigate for us, we don't have to think too much about it, just follow the instructions. Unreflectively following a healthy formula is a lot better than unreflectively following a whole bunch of unhealthy habits.

If we follow a measured and prescribed plan for life we may start to notice some benefits over time. What we might also notice is that we become far more aware of, or in touch with, ourselves. This leads us to option two. It is best, from a mindfulness perspective, to pay attention to our own minds and bodies, to the environment and to the day, and then to respond to what the present moment calls for. This is harder and it requires awareness and discernment, but ultimately it is the best. What we will probably find is that the best way to proceed is to use option one as a starting point and then transition to option two over time, as awareness and discernment grow.

Living our daily life healthily, happily and effectively requires attention, measure and balance.

A first principle is that virtually anything can be healthy or unhealthy depending on whether it is over- or underdone. As the ancient Greeks said, 'Nothing too much', otherwise translated as, 'Moderation in all things'. A second principle is that it is a lot easier if a family or household is on the same page in relation to measure. The best intentions are unlikely to last long if one family member is trying to lead a healthy and balanced life with the others doing the opposite. If you create a healthy atmosphere, make it a game, be creative and set challenges, it can be a family project that all can engage with.

What are some of the core elements we need to measure out in a healthy day and a healthy life? Here are a few key things.

EXERCISE

As a general guide, it's ideal to get around 20 to 30 minutes of vigorous exercise, such as jogging or tennis, on a daily basis, though on some days you'll do more and some days less. It is also good to vary the type of exercise you do. You might want to do more if training for something like a half-marathon or even a marathon, but this is a measure that is not optimal for sustainable health. You should also allow time for strength and flexibility training, as these aspects are equally important for our health.

Be aware of your body when you are exercising, because it will tell you everything you need to know. Exercise to a level where the body feels it is pushing itself, but not so much that it feels overstretched or traumatized. You want to finish with a sense of being healthily tired, not exhausted, unless of course you are young and training for some high-level performance. Of course there will be days you will slightly overdo it and days when you rest, especially if the body needs it. This will help you to find the right level for you and also to avoid injury. In terms of health and wellbeing, if you had to choose between exercising and having a few extra pounds, or not exercising and being a healthy weight, you would choose the exercise.

Find a time in the day that suits you best. If you are short on quality time with your children then exercise in such a way that it becomes time spent with your family — take a ball or frisbee to the park, go for a bike ride together or go for a walk to explore your neighbourhood.

FOOD

Being mindful with food has many benefits. Pay attention to the food choices you make when you are actually making them and then to your body when you are eating. Tasting the food as we eat it, and being present to the experience of eating, will not only help us to better enjoy the food but it will also help us to make more conscious food choices, and to pick up those messages the body gives when it has had enough; if we eat quickly and without attention, we miss that message and then it is too late. This can lead to consuming too many 'empty' (non-nutritious) calories which, over time, can lead to the development of chronic illnesses.

There is room for occasional indulgences, but if we are interested in reversing a chronic illness that is well underway then there is far less latitude for eating fatty and unnaturally sweet, empty calories devoid of fibre. In this situation we would need to stick to a healthy diet very closely. The Ornish program has been rigorously tested and found to be associated with reversal of heart disease and early cancer, and the reversal of the ageing process.[1,2,3] More than a diet, it is a whole lifestyle program, including meditation and group support.

WORK

As with everything else, too much or too little work is associated with poorer health. Of course, if you love your work you will tolerate working longer hours than someone who dislikes their work. However, even this can have its problems, especially if long work hours eat into time that should be spent with family, engaging in exercise or other interests. Time dedicated to work at the expense of a balanced life will start to negatively impact on the work itself, no matter how much we enjoy it. Taking time on a daily basis for self-care is an investment essential for working at a high level on a sustainable basis.

It is a wonderful thing to know when to stop working, not just at our place of work but at home as well. Pay attention, prioritize the jobs that really need doing, do them when it is time for them to be done and then stop when enough is enough. If we know when to stop then there will be enough time for other important parts of our day like self-care, sleep, meditation or leisure time. If we don't know when to stop and pay attention to these other important aspects of our lives, one day we will wind up talking to the boss or doctor about how to manage stress and burnout.

The other side of the coin is knowing when to start working. You will no doubt have had the experience of having enough time to get something done but instead deciding to put it off, to avoid it, procrastinate or find something else to do. Next thing you know the time has passed and the task hasn't been done. Then we suffer the effects of our procrastination — a letter from the taxation office because we didn't complete our tax forms on time; or water streaming down the internal walls of the house during a deluge because we didn't clear out the gutters when we should have. Take it as a general rule that there is always enough time for the things that really need to be done, but there is never enough time if we waste it or can't prioritize well.

Learn also to mindfully recognize the difference between not doing something or taking a break due to avoidance and procrastination, versus not doing it or having a break because that is what the moment requires. In the first instance we inwardly know we are not engaging with something that needs our attention, no matter how much our mind tries to justify otherwise. We will not feel at peace and the mind will keep returning to the task. In the second instance we will feel at peace, and the mind will be clear and can rest and rejuvenate We will be able to engage with what needs our attention at that time, whether it's a cup of tea or a different, more pressing job.

Another principle of mindful work is to use no more energy or force to do a task than is necessary. Measure out your use of energy with attention. For example, if we are not paying attention we often hold a pen with a vice-like grip, walk carrying tension that has no reason to be there or rush when we don't need to. Don't waste energy in this way, otherwise it won't be there when you really need it. Just like driving a car, drive it economically. When closing a cupboard or drawer, do it gently and with awareness. When stirring the tea or coffee use no more energy than is needed to do it. When hurrying and feeling pressured because the mind is getting ahead of itself, come back to the present moment and just take one step, or do one job, at a time.

LEISURE

We have discussed leisure already, but making sure we work it into our daily schedule will ensure that we take time for it. The thing is, if we fill up our day with work and allow no time for rest or creativity, then soon our work becomes unproductive and takes longer to get done. So learn to make time for leisure but, as with work, learn also when it is time to stop. If we are aware we will notice the quiet inward cue — 'Time to put that down now' — and will get back to what needs our attention. Help your children form good habits early in their lives: let them know when to turn off the computer, phone, tablet or other device.

SLEEP AND REST

For the majority of people 6 to 9 hours of nightly sleep is associated with optimal health, with those who meditate regularly generally needing less sleep than those who don't. Keep your bedtime and waking times regular, with occasional variation depending on the situation.

It is very helpful to have times of rest that are not about sleep. Punctuate the day with a minute here and there of mindfulness ('commas') or take 10 minutes at the end of a working day to sit, relax and listen to a soothing piece of music; or, if you drink wine, take time to really taste and savour the wine. Such pauses can be a great time to refresh and enliven ourselves, and will help us to conserve energy and to use it more wisely.

MEDITATION

It helps so much if we can carve out some time each day to meditate, to punctuate our day with 'full-stops'. We might practise for 5 minutes a day, but it's better if we can manage 10, 20, 40 or even 60 minutes a day. The more we put in the more we will benefit, but much more than 60 minutes a day and we had better consider joining a monastery. As with all things, know when enough is enough.

You might want to practise your meditation in one sitting or two. Twice a day is good because it bookends the main part of our day. It helps us to set ourselves up for the day ahead, and re-energize at the end of the working or school day.

Learning how to meditate is actually quite simple, but the main challenge is finding the time to do it. Actually, finding the time is not that hard — it's prioritizing the time for meditation that is the real challenge. Everything else gets in the way. The two main problems here are laziness and agitation: laziness in the form of apathy and inertia, where we don't have the energy or motivation to take the time to meditate; and agitation in the form of being unable to stop running with our addiction or compulsion to activity. However, if you really take the time to consider the cost of being unmindful this should help provide motivation. If you mentally factor in the time to meditate it will be there; if you leave it as an afterthought then it won't be. It's unlikely we will inscribe our tombstone with, 'I just wish I had another day at the office' but we might write, 'I wish I had taken more time to know myself.'

Measure the day as a family

There will be ways in which we measure out our day and our life that are particular to ourselves, our own needs and our own particular situation. It is important to also remember that it is far more helpful if there is a measure and flow to the life within the home shared by all those who live within it. For example, making the effort to cook together, share the family meal, exercise and meditate together, and do something creative together will help everyone to not only participate in healthy pursuits but will also help the family or housemates to connect. We don't just want a flow and rhythm to our own day, but also a flow and rhythm to the home itself.

Freedom versus measure

A fair question to ask is whether all this talk about measuring the day and the life smacks of regimentation? What about spontaneity? What about freedom?

The answer brings us back to mindfulness. Regimented or formulaic measures can be useful. They help a doctor treat a patient, and can help us to get a life back in order when things have become chaotic. Such measures help parents to assist children in adopting helpful habits; they help sporting teams to work as a unit and an army to work as a cohesive whole. They have their place and, if reasonable, can be mindful, useful and healthy.

Then there is unmindful regimentation that may not be reasonable and can be oppressive — doing something in a particular way or at a particular time when there is no rhyme nor reason to do so. Such an approach has the potential to be restrictive and create stress without any benefit. Mind you, sometimes there are useful habits that seem pointless and oppressive simply because we haven't yet recognized their reason or benefit. As stated in the movie *The Karate Kid*, 'Wax on, wax off'.

The mindful way to effectively measure is known in the moment. Ask yourself: what is needed in this moment? It could be that we really do need a rest day from our exercise schedule or that we need to stay up a bit later to complete an important job. It might be that we leave mowing the lawn today in order to go to the movies with our children. Or perhaps we forego watching the football on television one afternoon because the tax just has to be done. Spontaneity is the very essence of mindfulness, as is the mindful application of discipline, because it is all about the needs of the present moment. This leads to freedom and is the very expression of it.

Measuring the budget

One very important part of life that needs to be measured carefully is the household budget. With care and attention limited finances can go a long way. Without care and attention we can squander a lot of money in a short time.

First, it is mindful to be able to distinguish between needs and wants. Wants often masquerade as needs and can lead us to spend much more than would be prudent. Too many wants too much of the time soon turns to greed and dissatisfaction, which is the Achilles heel that unscrupulous financial advisors look for and manipulate. The thing that leads us to pursue our wants far in excess of our needs is attachment. Letting go or not being so attached to possessions and desires helps free us from such a potential bind.

Second, it is helpful to live well within our means if at all possible. If we needlessly stretch our resources to the limit then we will leave very little latitude to cope with unexpected events. As a result our financial position will be fragile and constantly on the edge of a potential crisis. This also includes borrowing comfortably within our limits while assuming that the financial environment might change. If it changes for the better then well and good, but if it changes for the worse we should still be able to adapt.

Taking a mindful approach to finances can help us recognize when to pull out of a situation like a poor investment. Mindfulness has been shown to help protect people from what is known as the sunk-cost bias: 'the tendency to continue an endeavour once an investment in money, effort or time has been made'.[4]

Lastly, buy the best quality you can afford. The cheapest option is often far more expensive in terms of money, time and inconvenience in the long run.

On a practical level, it is very helpful to practise some mindfulness when confronted by a significant financial or purchasing decision. See what presents and see if you can discern what is motivating you to move in one direction or another. Make the choice wisely — mindfully.

Connection

We have spent our time discussing ways to foster mindfulness within our home; now it is time to broaden our view and look at what it means to be mindfully connected, not just within the home but beyond the boundaries of our own front door.

When the word 'connected' is used these days it is generally associated with technology such as the internet, Skype, social media and the like. If used well, these can be excellent methods of staying in touch with others and accessing the information, goods and services we need to live. Some people feel they can't live without these modes of electronic connection and are perhaps too dependent on them. Paradoxically, this can lead to a form of isolation and a loss of social skills. Others are not so dependent and are masters, rather than slaves, of the technology. It is possible to be mindful and electronically connected at the same time.

Perhaps more direct and mindful is the connectedness that comes with a sense of community, through knowing the people in your street, shopping at your local shops, being involved in community projects and activities, being socially aware and engaging in social issues.

Interacting directly, face to face, with family and friends and our wider community is a basic human need. The internet can facilitate this but it can't replace it.

Connection is good for health

Our social, mental and physical health are intimately related. If one is good then the others are more likely to be good. Of all the things that predict the wellbeing of adolescents, connectedness at home and school comes out on top.[5] Good social and emotional health, among other things, is associated with less heart disease, better immunity, a healthier brain and less anxiety and depression. One study exploring the relationship between connectedness and happiness concluded: 'People's happiness depends on the happiness of others with whom they are connected. This provides further justification for seeing happiness, like health, as a collective phenomenon.'[6]

Social isolation, on the other hand, is associated with higher death rates and lower life expectancy independent of other lifestyle factors.[7] Social factors associated with better health and lower death rates include marriage (unless very unhappily married) and stable long-term cohabiting relationships, contact with family and friends, religious or spiritual affiliation, and being affiliated with community groups.

SOCIAL INTERACTION AND SOLITUDE

Whether we want more or less interaction with others is an individual measure. Someone who is more extroverted will want and need more time for social interaction than someone who is more introverted, who will prefer more time for solitude and introspection. Each have their strengths and weaknesses. An extrovert can crave interaction and the validation of others to the point that they become alienated from themselves and cannot comfortably sit in stillness and solitude, even for a short time. In this case being with yourself feels like a kind of death. It's very revealing. An introvert, on the other hand, can easily become isolated and withdrawn if they are not careful, to the point that social interaction is uncomfortable and even threatening.

If we are around people all the time and are not taking time to sit and just be, then make time. If we are withdrawing and avoiding interaction then make the effort to get out and interact. When either pattern gets entrenched it gets more and more difficult to snap out of. Ideally we want to be able to move comfortably into social situations and then feel equally comfortable with a period of solitude.

Solitude and isolation, however, are two different things. Solitude is a basic human need; isolation is not. In solitude we feel at one, and connected although we are physically alone. In isolation we feel cut off and disconnected, even if we are in a room with a hundred people. Both are the result of an internal state of mind, not the outward circumstances.

HOW TO INCREASE CONNECTION

Knowing your neighbours is a good place to start. Chat over the fence, offer to feed their pets or water their gardens when they are away, catch up for drinks from time to time, and send some fruit their way when your fruit trees are cropping. You don't need to manufacture situations; just be ready to respond to the situations that naturally arise.

There are other simple ways of increasing the connectedness between home, our community and the world outside the home. We can go for a walk or run in the neighbourhood on a regular basis. Mind you, when walking you are much more likely to stop and chat than if you are jogging. Walking the dog makes chatting to neighbours almost unavoidable.

Shopping locally is also good. Your local store might not offer the best prices, but that's not the point. You will not only be spending time in your own neighbourhood but also financially supporting local people and businesses. Local sporting clubs provide a great way for adults to meet peers of a similar age when their children are playing in the same sporting teams. And community projects, such as caring for the local parks and environment, joining a community garden, working for community infrastructure projects and raising funds for community charities all increase the social capital.

Spending time with friends and family is possibly the most important form of connection. We thrive on the warmth and goodwill of their company. We don't need to live in each other's pockets nor do we need masses of friends to be connected. The depth of the relationships is more important than the volume of them — think quality over quantity. Being present and engaged — remaining mindful — when spending time with those closest to us will ensure that quality.

Participating in hobbies, sports and classes are a few of the many ways we can connect with people with whom we are likely to have something in common. This makes meeting others much easier and helps to oil the wheels of social interactions.

Connection doesn't stop with our local community but expands as far as we care to take it. We might be involved, or want to be involved, with causes on a state, national or international scale. You may be donating to non-government aid organizations, sponsoring a child in a developing country, choosing to only eat foods farmed in environmentally sensitive ways or lending your voice to public debate. Travel also opens our eyes and connects us to our world on a much larger scale. We will each do it in our own way. If children are brought up to connect in such ways then they will be well prepared for a happier and more useful life.

To be mindful means to be aware, to engage and to respond. To be mindful is to be at one with ourselves and to be at one with, and to connect to, the world around us. Then we can be at home wherever we are.

Final thought

As John Donne wrote, 'No man is an island.' Obviously no woman or child is either — and nor is the home an island. No matter what we think, we do not live in isolation. None of us is totally self-sufficient. There is interdependence between people living in neighbourhoods, communities, towns, cities, states and nations. Connection is the very lifeblood of humanity and the home.

Mindfulness Meditation

mindfulness
meditation

Like a book, a day that's not punctuated makes no sense. The formal practice of mindfulness is meditation. If the meditation lasts for a few minutes or more then it can be likened to a 'full-stop' in the day. Supplementing these 'full-stops', regular, short mindful pauses during the day — of anywhere from a few seconds to a couple of minutes — might be compared to 'commas'.

A good 'starting dose' for those who are new to mindfulness is to practise meditation for 5 minutes twice daily. Before breakfast and dinner are good times, as after food is a low point for the metabolism and sleep can occur more easily then (which might be a good power nap but it's not mindfulness meditation). The duration of practice can be built up to 10, then 15, 20 and even up to 30 minutes or longer if required, depending on your time availability, motivation, needs and commitment.

If you forget to meditate at the optimal time then practise when you remember and have the opportunity. Meditation reminder apps, for both phones and computers, are available if you wish to use them. If your day is full of unavoidable emergencies, then simply practise when you have finished dealing with them.

'Commas' during the day can help to reinforce our ability to be mindful for the whole of our day, including when we're not meditating. Even pausing only for long enough to take a couple of deep breaths can help us break our mindless build-up of tension and mental activity. A good time to practise 'commas' is when we're between activities. For example, you might have just finished work and are in the car, ready to drive home — just take a few moments to be mindful. Or perhaps you've just arrived home and you might take a few moments in the car before going into the house. Or you might have just completed one job and are about to pick up another; just take a few moments to put some space between jobs. If you are just about to go into an interview, take a few moments to be present before walking into the room. Or perhaps you could take a few moments before eating your lunch, to prepare the mind to taste the food and not just bolt it down without enjoying it or even being aware of what you're eating.

For our longer practices of mindfulness meditation — our 'full-stops' — it can be helpful, wherever possible, to have a quiet place to practise without interruption. However, this doesn't mean that mindfulness can't be practised anywhere, any time — indeed, it's important for the practice to be as 'portable' as possible. When practising for longer periods, interruptions will inevitably occur. If this happens, it helps to not be concerned but rather just deal with the interruption mindfully and then, if possible, go back to the practice. When sitting down to practise it helps to have a clock within easy view to help reduce anxiety about time. Just open your eyes when you think the meditation time might be up, and if the time's not up yet simply move back into the practice. An alarm can be useful but make sure it's one that won't jolt you out of meditation.

Now we can move on to the formal practice of mindfulness by using the sense of touch, focused on the body and/or breath. We can also use another sense, such as hearing, or a combination of senses. The important thing about the body and the senses is that they are always operating in the present moment, so they help to bring our mind into the present moment if we pay attention to them — this is what 'coming to our senses' means. Contact with any of the senses will automatically unhook the attention from the mental distractions which otherwise hijack our attention.

Position

A seated position is generally preferred as you are less likely to go to sleep if upright, and we're somewhat constrained in what we can achieve when we're not conscious! In sitting for meditation it's best if your back and neck are straight and balanced, which requires a minimum of effort or tension to maintain the position. A meditation stool is a small stool without a back rest, which helps the spine find its natural position. Lying down can also be useful, particularly if deep physical relaxation is the main aim of the practice or if the body is extremely tired, in pain or ill. However, the ease of going to sleep while lying down might not always be desirable, unless it's late at night or you need a power nap.

Having settled into your preferred meditating position, it's usual to let the eyes gently close. You can practise with eyes open, as the Dalai Lama does, but closing our eyes can help bring the other senses, which we tend to underutilize, into play. Now you are ready to meditate.

The body scan

The body scan is the most widely used and generally the best mindfulness practice to begin with. Begin by being conscious of your whole body and letting it settle. Now, progressively become aware of each individual part of the body, starting with the feet. Let the attention rest there a while, feeling whatever there is to be felt. Then let the attention move to the legs, stomach, back, hands, arms, shoulders, neck and face, pausing for a while at each point. Take your time with each body part — how much time you intend to

dedicate to the total practice will determine how long you spend with each individual part.

The object of this practice is to let the attention rest with each body part, simply noticing what's happening there, what sensations are taking place, moment by moment. Even if there's a relative lack of sensation in one or other part of the body we simply notice that lack of sensation. In the process we naturally practise cultivating an attitude of impartial awareness — that is, not having to judge experiences as good or bad, right or wrong. Nor do we need to cling to the aspects of meditation we like or that are pleasant and push away those aspects we don't like or that are uncomfortable. Learning to cultivate equanimity

and the ability to be at peace with the present moment is a core aspect of mindfulness practice.

It's helpful to practise being at ease with our moment-by-moment experience just as it is, even if it's uncomfortable. As mentioned, it's simple but not necessarily easy. We may soon discover that it's our reactivity to emotional and physical discomfort which amplifies both our experience of it and the suffering it produces. There's no need to change your experience from one state to another or to 'make something happen'. Our state will change from moment to moment without us having to do anything — we just flow with it.

Judgment, criticism, worry and distraction, for example, are simply mental experiences, like physical sensations, to observe non-judgmentally as they come and go. As often as the attention wanders from awareness of the body, simply notice where it has gone and gently bring it back to an awareness of the part of the body you are up to. It's not a problem that thoughts come in or that the mind gets distracted; it only becomes a problem if we make it a problem.

A sense of clarity or insight often arises during meditation, which might lead to a temptation to race off and start planning things or sorting out problems. As tempting as this might be, defer such activities until after the practice is over and then use the mindful state for useful work. Let the transition from formal mindfulness meditation in stillness to mindful activity be seamless.

Although it might not be obvious to us throughout formal mindfulness practice, we are not only practising attention. We are also practising qualities such as an attitude of acceptance, a spirit of inquiry, equanimity, patience and even courage. When we practise these qualities in the chair we soon start to find that we take a bit of them with us when we get out of the chair.

Learn to be at peace with the present moment

Breathing

Meditation focusing on the breath tends to be the next form of mindfulness meditation to be learnt and practised. Just as the attention can be rested on the sense of touch through the body, the attention can be rested with the breath as it passes in and out of the body. The point of focus could be right where the air enters and leaves through the nose, or it could be where the stomach rises and falls with the breath.

Just as in the body scan, no force is required to be mindfully aware of the breath, and in mindfulness mediation there's no need to try to regulate the breathing; let the body do that for you. It's pretty good at it if we don't keep interfering with it. Just think about how many times you've forgotten to breathe after going to sleep and still woken up alive and well the next morning! Again, if distracting thoughts and feelings come into awareness (carrying the attention away with them like a pirate with our real treasure) just be aware of them but let them come and go by themselves. There's no need to 'battle' with these thoughts or to 'get rid' of them. There's no need even to try to stop these thoughts coming into the mind, or to try to force them out. Trying to force thoughts and feelings out of our minds just feeds them

with what they thrive on — attention — which makes them stronger and increases their impact. We're simply practising being less preoccupied with them or reactive to them. They will settle by themselves and all the more quickly if we learn not to get involved in them. Like trains of thought we don't have to fight with the trains, nor do we need to get on them.

Listening

We can also use listening to mindfully meditate — the practice of restful attentiveness is similar to the body scan and breathing. Here we're simply practising being conscious of the sounds in our environment, whether they are close or far away. As we listen, let the sounds come and go and in the process also let any thoughts about the sounds (or about anything else for that matter) come and go. Keep gently bringing the attention back to the present when it wanders.

Sooner or later it tends to dawn on us that most of the time we are listening to mental chatter, so the value of listening mindfully is that the attention is not being used to feed the usual mental commentary. It is this commentary that is so full of habitual and unconscious rumination, worries and negative self-talk.

ENDNOTES

CHAPTER 2

1. http://time.com/1556/the-mindful-revolution/

2. sfinsight.org/MindfulRevolutionTIME.pdf

3. Hallowell, E.M. 2005, 'Overloaded circuits: Why smart people underperform,' *Harv Bus Rev*, Jan:83(1):54–62, 116.

4. McEvoy, S.P., Stevenson, M.R. and Woodward, M. 2007, 'The contribution of passengers versus mobile phone use to motor vehicle crashes resulting in hospital attendance by the driver', *Accid Anal Prev*, Nov:39(6):1170–6.

5. http://ucsdcfm.wordpress.com/2011/07/01/our-brains-are-evolving-to-multitask-not-the-ill-usion-of-multitasking/

6. Foerde, K., Knowlton, B.J. and Poldrack, R.A. 2006, 'Modulation of competing memory systems by distraction', *Proc Natl Acad Sci USA*, August 1: 103(31):11778–83, doi: 10.1073/pnas.0602659103.

CHAPTER 3

1. http://en.wikipedia.org/wiki/New_Classical_architecture

2. Johnson, A. 1999, *Famous Problems and Their Mathematicians*, Libraries Unlimited, Santa Barbara, p. 45: 'The Golden Ratio is a standard feature of many modern designs, from postcards and credit cards to posters and light-switch plates.'

CHAPTER 6

1. Selander, J. et al. 2013, 'Joint effects of job strain and road-traffic and occupational noise on myocardial infarction', *Scand J Work Environ Health*, Mar 1:39(2):195–203. doi: 10.5271/sjweh.3324.

2. Röösli M. 2013, 'Health effects of environmental noise exposure', *Ther Umsch*, Dec:70(12):720–4. doi: 10.1024/0040-5930/a000470.

3. Bakker, R.H. et al. 2012 'Impact of wind turbine sound on annoyance, self-reported sleep disturbance and psychological distress', *Sci Total Environ*, May 15:425:42–51. doi: 10.1016/j.scitotenv.2012.03.005.

4. Hill, E.M., Billington, R. and Krägeloh, C. 2014, 'Noise sensitivity and diminished health: Testing moderators and mediators of the relationship', *Noise Health*, Jan–Feb:16(68):47–56. doi: 10.4103/1463-1741.127855.

5. Kreuzer, P.M. et al. 2012, 'Mindfulness-and body-psychotherapy-based group treatment of chronic tinnitus: A randomized controlled pilot study', *BMC Complement Altern Med*, Nov 28:12:235. doi: 10.1186/1472-6882-12-235.

6. Hesser, H., Molander, P., Jungermann, M. and Andersson, G. 2013, 'Costs of suppressing emotional sound and countereffects of a mindfulness induction: An experimental analog of tinnitus impact', *PLoS One*, May 10:8(5):e64540. doi: 10.1371/journal.pone.0064540.

7. Philippot, P. et al. 2012, 'A randomized controlled trial of mindfulness-based cognitive therapy for treating tinnitus', *Clin Psychol Psychother*, Sep:19(5):411–9. doi: 10.1002/cpp.756.

8. McCraty, R., Barrios-Choplin, B., Atkinson, M. and Tomasino, D. 1998, 'The effects of different types of music on mood, tension, and mental clarity', *Alt Therapies in Health and Medicine*, 4(1):75–84.

9. Wilson, T.D. et al. 2014, 'Just think: The challenges of the disengaged mind', *Science*, 4 July:345(6192):75–7. doi: 10.1126/science.1250830.

CHAPTER 9

1. Jacka, F.N. et al. 2010, 'Associations between diet quality and depressed mood in adolescents: Results from the Australian Healthy Neighbourhoods Study', *Aust NZ J Psychiatry*, May:44(5):435–42.

2. Resnick, M.D. et al. 1997 'Protecting adolescents from harm: Findings from the National Longitudinal Study on Adolescent Health', *JAMA*, Sep 10;278(10):823–32.

3. Dalen, J. et al. 2010, 'Pilot study: Mindful Eating and Living (MEAL): Weight, eating behavior, and psychological outcomes associated with a mindfulness-based intervention for people with obesity', *Complement Ther Med*, Dec:18(6):260–4.

CHAPTER 10

1. Landau, S.M. et al. 2012, 'Association of lifetime cognitive engagement and low -amyloid deposition', *Arch Neurol*, Jan 23.

2. Simic, G., Babic, M., Borovecki, F. and Hof, P.R. 2014, 'Early failure of the default-mode network and the pathogenesis of Alzheimer's disease', *CNS Neurosci Ther*, Apr 8. doi: 10.1111/cns.12260.

3. Hölzel, B.K. et al. 2011, 'Mindfulness practice leads to increases in regional brain gray matter density', *Psychiatry Res*, Jan 30:191(1):36–43.

4. http://news.harvard.edu/gazette/story/2011/01/eight-weeks-to-a-better-brain/

5. Brewer, J.A. et al. 2011, 'Meditation experience is associated with differences in default mode network activity and connectivity', *Proc Natl Acad Sci USA*, Dec 13:108(50):20254–9.

6. Zeidan, F. et al. 2010, 'Mindfulness meditation improves cognition: Evidence of brief mental training', *Conscious Cogn*, Jun:19(2):597–605.

7. Friedland, R.P. et al. 2001, 'Patients with Alzheimer's disease have reduced activities in midlife compared with healthy control-group members', *Proceedings of the National Academy of Science USA*, 10.1073/pnas.061002998.

8. Scarmeas, N. et al. 2001, 'Influence of leisure activity on the incidence of Alzheimer's disease', *Neurology*, 57(12):2236–42.

9. Verghese, J. et al. 2003, 'Leisure activities and the risk of dementia in the elderly', *New England Journal of Medicine*, 348(25):2508–16.

10. American Academy of Pediatrics, Committee on Public Education 2001, 'Children, adolescents and television', *Pediatrics*, 107:423–6.

11. Straker, L.M., Abbott, R.A. and Smith, A.J. 2013, 'To remove or to replace traditional electronic games? A crossover randomised controlled trial on the impact of removing or replacing home access to electronic games on physical activity and sedentary behaviour in children aged 10–12 years', *BMJ Open*, 3(6): e002629, June 11. doi: 10.1136/bmjopen-2013-002629.

CHAPTER 15

1. http://www.allergy.org.au/images/stories/aer/infobulletins/2010pdf/AER_Asthma_and_Allergy.pdf

2. http://www.allergy.org.au/ascia-reports/allergy-and-immune-diseases-in-australia-2013

3. http://www.allergy.org.au/health-professionals/hp-information/asthma-and-allergy/aeroallergen-avoidance-is-it-worthwhile

4. http://ntn.org.au/wp/wp-content/uploads/2010/02/children_paper08.pdf

5. http://www.epa.gov/iaq/voc.html.

CHAPTER 16

1. Wachernagel, M. and Rees, W. 1996, *Our Ecological Footprint: Reducing human impact on the Earth*, New Society Publishers, Gabriola Island, BC.

2. de Graaf, J., Wann, D. and Naylor, T.H. 2001, *Affluenza: The all-consuming epidemic*, Berrett-Koehler Publishers, San Francisco.

CHAPTER 17

1. Ornish, D. et al. 1990, 'Can lifestyle changes reverse coronary heart disease? The Lifestyle Heart Trial', *Lancet*, Jul 21:336(8708):129–33.

2. Ornish, D. et al. 2005, 'Intensive lifestyle changes may affect the progression of prostate cancer', *J Urol*, Sep:174(3):1065–9; discussion 1069–70.

3. Ornish, D. et al. 2013, 'Effect of comprehensive lifestyle changes on telomerase activity and telomere length in men with biopsy-proven low-risk prostate cancer: 5-year follow-up of a descriptive pilot study', *Lancet Oncol*, Sep 16. doi:pii: S1470–2045(13)70366–8. 10.1016/S1470–2045(13)70366–8.

4. Hafenbrack, A.C., Kinias, Z. and Barsade, S.G. 2014, 'Debiasing the mind through meditation: Mindfulness and the sunk-cost bias', *Psychological Science*, vol. 25(2) 369–76.

5. Resnick, M.D. et al. 1997, 'Protecting adolescents from harm: Findings from the National Longitudinal Study on Adolescent Health', *JAMA*, Sep 10:278(10):823–32.

6. Fowler, J.H. and Christakis, N.A. 2008, 'Dynamic spread of happiness in a large social network: Longitudinal analysis over 20 years in the Framingham Heart Study', *BMJ*, Dec 4:337:a2338. doi: 10.1136/bmj.a2338.

7. House, J.S., Landis, K.R. and Umberson, D. 1988, 'Social relationships and health', *Science*, Jul 29:241(4865):540–5.

Index

First published 2015

Exisle Publishing Pty Ltd
'Moonrising', Narone Creek Road, Wollombi, NSW 2325, Australia
P.O. Box 60–490, Titirangi, Auckland 0642, New Zealand
www.exislepublishing.com

A CiP record for this book is available from the National Library of Australia.

ISBN 978-1-921966-81-1

Design and typesetting by Mark Thacker of Big Cat Design
Typeset in Sabon 9.65 on 14.5pt
Printed in China

This book uses paper sourced under ISO 14001 guidelines from well-managed forests and
other controlled sources.

2 4 6 8 10 9 7 5 3 1

Disclaimer
While this book is intended as a general information resource and all care has been
taken in compiling the contents, neither the author nor the publisher and their distributors
can be held responsible for any loss, claim or action that may arise from reliance on the
information contained in this book.